# I Forgive You, Daddy – Yoga and the Angels Healed Me!

## Along with Astrology, Channeling, Dreams, Past-Life Recall, Psychicism, Telepathy, Walk-Ins and the Whales

Michelle Star

Printed by CreateSpace, An Amazon.com Company

Available from Amazon.com, CreateSpace.com, and other retail outlets

Available on Kindle and online stores

# DEDICATION

To the One, the Source of all being and creativity--the One from whom my creativity flows and the One to whom my creativity returns in the Circle of Life. To all the guides, angels, extra-terrestrial and human beings that have shared their knowledge, ability and love, I hereby request Spirit to return your kindness and generosity a thousand-fold.

Love brings unity by healing the split between the body and the heart. When the body and heart unite, one merges with the soul like countless rivers and streams merge into the vast ocean. Love is the only worldwide religion.

Bapuji (Kripaluvananda)

All adversity is bathed in the Love of God. There is Divine design in every adversity… what is the lesson?

"In Touch Ministry" Radio Program

Forgiveness is the economy of the heart… forgiveness saves the expense of anger, the cost of hatred, the waste of spirits.

Hanna More

# CONTENTS

# ACKNOWLEDGMENTS

There are many that have provided assistance in the 24 years I have written and re-written this book. But first, I must acknowledge my family for providing the backdrop for my life of growth and depth; my Mother, Father and Big Sis, Vickie and to my twin brother for his sharing in our close bond.

I must give many thanks and appreciation to those that helped with editing and uncovering my "voice" in this work: Judith C. Amburgey-Peters, my friend and professor at the College of Wooster, Department of Chemistry, we share many similarities; Michelle Martin, ED.S., School Psychologist and Founder/Director of Insight Learning & Wellness Center whose patience and grounding sets a fine example for me to emulate. There are those that have contributed in a financial way that has kept me afloat at times and allowed me to pursue my dreams and follies: thank you, Ann Jordan, we share angel energy in our Reiki sessions; John S. who remains private and has gone far above and beyond the call of friendship with his generosity and patience—my kitties and I thank you many times over.

Many students have contributed to my dream too by allowing me to offer early morning Yoga and sessions in Reiki, and by becoming my friends: Wendy Lapsevich, Raymond Banyas, Ellie Jisa and Sheila Maurer, and, of course, Allyson Grills and the Yoga Club over the past eight years.

A thank you too, Daniel and Cindy at SAGA, for your patience and professionalism.

# 1 INTRODUCTION

The Center for Disease Control states that as of their January 2014 update, suicide is the third leading cause of death among youths and young adults aged 10 to 24 years in the United States. Deaths from suicide are only part of the problem since more young people survive suicide attempts than actually die. Boys are more likely than girls to die from suicide, but girls are more likely to report their attempts than boys. Alcohol and drugs exacerbate the problem. There are many possible causes of suicide, depression being one of the more prominent.

In 1970, I might have become one of these statistics. At age 23, I reached the point where life was too much of a challenge and made an attempt to end my life. This event and the subsequent emotional healing I experienced have ignited a passion within me to help others who feel they live a life of "quiet desperation" or otherwise cannot find lasting happiness. Through the use of tools like Yoga, meditation, dream work, and psychic or intuitive development, I have found amazing peace and strength. It was always here, within me, it was just buried under oppressive pounds of pain and anguish.

Since the writing of the *Yoga Sutras of Patanjali* 2000 years ago and up to the present time, volumes have been written about Yoga, giving instruction on how to practice the asanas or postures, breathing, and meditation. Many techniques have been offered through the written word to teach seekers how to achieve physical skill, strength and flexibility, mental/emotional balance, and peace of mind. I will not be reiterating the physical postures of Hatha Yoga here, however, I proffer the practice of Yoga and meditation has been the underpinning of my process, growth, and healing. Nearly on a daily basis, I offer my gratitude to the ancients who created Yoga and to the Source that inspired them. The body/mind is like a four-lane highway and

Yoga a road map to the destination of healing, wholeness, and Unity consciousness.

What this book offers are stories and teachings from someone who has lived through the experience of a suicide attempt, followed by the descent into the depths of darkness, the unconscious mind. I subsequently found and practiced Yoga and meditation, psychic development and dream work for four and a half decades to heal my deep, underlying issues. Truth be known, Yoga found me.

You will find not only some of the physiological benefits of Yoga and meditation which are supported by scientific research (hopefully, prompting your own exploration and practice), but also some examples of the spiritual growth and psychic opening that may arise through such practice depending on the level of commitment and interest, talent and ability of the seeker. Ultimately, these practices offer the hope of lifting one up out of the mire of depression and ignorance—turning inside out, going into the dark to find Light. Life becomes very interesting, indeed.

Another question which this writing may serve to answer for some is this: how do I heal when I do not know or remember what happened to cause the depression, low self-esteem, self-destructive behaviors, and suicidal tendencies? Some prefer to let sleeping dogs lie, but I believe behavioral and emotional patterns, irrational fears, and depression all stem from somewhere. The causes might not even have occurred in this lifetime. They might be recorded deep in the soul—insidiously hidden. How does one find answers, and how does one resolve or heal the issues?

Exploring further, just what happens to a person who practices Yoga and meditation for a long time? This book describes experiences showing the opening and connecting of mind and body to a more expansive reality with a spiritual foundation. In writing it, actually, in *living* it, I feel like I have "turned myself inside out," as the journey took me into the "womb of the Goddess" or the "belly of the whale" and back out again into the Light. (More description of this descent is written in Joseph Campbell's book, *The Hero with a Thousand Faces.*) Some of these stories may raise the hair on the back of your neck, possibly causing a head-on collision with some of your more commonly held beliefs. I am not intending to persuade anyone to change their beliefs, unless they see fit, of course. My hope is that the reader will merely open to the possibility that others walking a "road less traveled" may have a piece of the puzzle too, or another part of Truth to share, and ultimately develop tolerance and compassion for those on a different path. All paths inevitably lead back to the same Source/Creator.

It is my intent also to share useful information, techniques and my personal experience, which may offer hope and provide help with healing breaches and glitches in one's inner connections. I hope to promote Unity Consciousness—now knowing the Oneness that we are.

In the very least, I have given hints as to how one might approach attaining peace of mind. This is my contribution to assist in and intention for creating a more peaceful world. Peace begins within each person—and I quote the lyrics sung at the conclusion of services at Unity Church, "Let there be peace on Earth, and let it begin with me."

Shanti (Peace),

*Michelle Star*
September 1, 2014

# 2 Curse of the Night – The Doorway of Memory Cracks Open

When we were 4 years old, my twin brother and I still slept in separate cribs in our shared bedroom. It would be one more year before individual twin beds replaced our respective cribs, and we were moved into our own rooms. Our parents were caught off guard when we were born—back then, in 1946, tests were not performed to detect multiple fetuses—we presented a two-for-one set as a surprise!

Our family lived in an Ohio cheese and dairy farm community with a population of about 3,000. Located about three blocks from the center of town, our house was small and covered in grey shingles. Our town had only one traffic light.

My father left Hawaii to come home from his tour of duty in the Navy in 1945 near the end of World War II. My mother had endured three years *sans* husband, caring for her hyperactive daughter, my sister, who arrived just before our new sailor-father left for the naval seas. These were turbulent times where depression and war stories prevailed, but at least mother and baby daughter had the support of family living in our home town. My twin brother and I arrived about nine months after our father returned, in 1946, as did so many other full-fledged members of the Baby Boomer generation.

It was during our fourth year that I awoke in the night, sitting up in my crib, wanting to escape the man who was standing, leering, on a ladder tilted against the outside of our single bedroom window. I knew he was trying to get at me. I screamed and cried until our mother came running. Assuming I merely had a nightmare, she tried to talk me down from my tears of terror. Why would she not believe he had been there? I *saw* him. His eyes ogled me; I could sense his evil intention through his looming large, dark shape, framed by the outline of the window. I could see eyes, face and broad shoulders. But I felt there was no escape from him—only escape during waking hours—for now. This is the first memory of my life and the first of dozens of near nightly vivid experiences where I woke up the entire household screaming and crying in hysterics. After a while, I did not want to go to bed at night and insisted the hall light be left on until I finally fell asleep. Sometimes, even the sound of our mother eventually flipping the light switch off would trigger a hyper vigilant reaction of panic and screams. Incredible stress, it was troubling for such a young child. Sometimes, I would jump out of bed, landing out of reach of any monsters lurking under the bed, and dash down the stairs, racing the ghosts to my parents' bed. That choice, made in spite of being the lesser of two evils: getting squashed between two hot adults or lying alone in cold fear. Reflecting through older eyes, these experiences seemed more like an alternate reality than lucid dreams or nightmares. They continued for several years.

As I lay awake in bed one night, my parents appeared standing together in the doorway to my room. I was about eight years old and still experiencing the scream-dreams causing everyone in the household to awaken and rush to my room. When they first began at four years old, they did not seem like dreams to me. They were incredibly real, and the terror they stabbed into me stuck well into my waking state. After a while though, we passed them off as common nightmares. But on this particular night, my parents stood side-by-side in a uniquely united front, holding our family's Christmas tree-top angel. The angel was donned with a full-length, indigo gown and held a transparent magic wand. When she was connected to electric current, light radiated through her gown, up into her face and down to the five-pointed star on the end of her wand held in her left hand. She brought a magical calm to the night. The angel night light was left on in my room to stand guard over me and hold the monsters of the night at bay. I resisted sleep, gazing at her as though tapping into the very angels she represented. Ultimately, I would surrender to slumber. I think that was probably one of the most heartwarming things my parents ever did for me. I was grateful for their thoughtfulness. Finally, after several years of being chased, running frantically from some man or other assortment of inner ghosts, I felt safe enough to sleep. The nightmares stopped—for a while.

I was a highly sensitive child, unable to bear loud noises, which was torture as there were a lot of family arguments, and sensitive feelings that were hurt easily with just a glare from our mother. I did possess a fiery temper that according to family tales was riled when my movements of exploration were restricted; I nonetheless appeared to demonstrate a capacity for caring and compassion at an early age. I walked at the age of eight months, where my twin brother crawled until he was 12 months, not unusual for fraternal boy-girl twins. (He was born second in line and was smaller than me weighing a mere 4 pounds at birth.) When I accidentally stepped on his fingers in my race to learn about the world, I would stoop down next to my sobbing brother, caressing him and cooing, "It's okay, Buddy, I sorry! Everything will be aw wight!" But the conditions of my life would squelch that naturally nurturing personality until I reached the age of 23. The plastic angel by my bed with her magic wand could not prevent the events that molded me into an emotionally disturbed young lady. She soothed me and helped me endure the nights. What I needed was help with my days.

# 3 STILL FIVE AND TAKING CHARGE

Life's challenges intensified while my brother and I were still five years old. We now enjoyed our own rooms as though part of a normal rite of passage. I remember my mother's considerate approach as we stood in the upstairs hall where she offered me my own room and twin bed. She kneeled down at my eye level and explained that I had a choice whether or not to sleep in my own room and asked if I was ready. I answered without hesitation that I was. I took my grey, musical stuffed elephant and moved down the hall.

Sometime later, but while we were still five years old, my mother began to change. There always seemed to be an abundance of family arguments, some spanking and punishments, but things took a turn for the worse. Now my twin and I were summoned to the bathroom on a daily basis. Behind closed doors, we were required to lower our clothing below the waist, one at a time bend over the commode exposing our bottoms and submit to a spanking--for no reason. At least no reason we could figure out. At first I cried, not only because it was physically painful, but I felt confused, hurt and disappointed. I do not know how long we endured that treatment, perhaps only a couple of weeks. But I remember how the yardsticks, props holding up the windows, and rulers would break over our behinds. Then we would dutifully search the house for a new tool to assist our mother on her mission. If there was no tool, she used her hand in one of those "this will hurt me more than it hurts you" type scenarios. Eventually, I learned to suppress my tears as I grew weary of crying, and I did not want to give my mother the satisfaction. Finally, much to our gratitude and relief, our eight and a half year old sister yelled from another room of the house, "Will you stop beating those twins! " Our mother seemed to awaken to what she was

7

doing as she exclaimed, "Oh! " The daily ritual stopped. In retrospect years later, my imagination caused me to wonder if the Divine Mother intervened mimicking the voice of my sister. My sister was rarely home. It seemed as though she would disappear and reappear out of nowhere since I never knew where she went. Perhaps she escaped to our aunt's house which was within walking distance. Whether the words were actually spoken or sent through the voice of the unseen, I was truly grateful for the relief from physical assault. The impact on my self-esteem, however, would take a tad longer to repair.

Within a day or two, the three of us kids stood outside the bathroom door talking about our mother's noticeable change in behavior. My wise older sister stated she thought our mother was "sick." I piped up with a "Yes! " in agreement recognizing truth in her assessment. At that moment, I experienced what I would later discover was an intuitive flash impressing upon me that I was going to live to be over a hundred years old and the first half of my life would be "really hard," and the second half would be "very nice", in the words of a child. I felt a light pressure on the right side of my head over my brain and then just "knew" this.

Years later, we learned that our mother had a uterine fibroid tumor the size of an orange when she was pregnant with my brother and me. While still in the hospital after delivering us, she began to hemorrhage and was taken into emergency surgery. She explained later to us that while on the operating table, she floated up to a corner of the ceiling. She looked down on herself and the medical team attending to her surgery. My mother's heart had stopped on the operating table—she died. Still aware of herself from the ceiling, she felt peaceful and wanted to stay, but also felt compelled to return since she had babies that needed her care. The doctor removed the tumor, but also performed a complete hysterectomy. She was only 23 years old, and in a few years, she plunged into premature menopause and depression. (There is that age again--23.) This was an account we heard repeated so often, we eventually accepted and internalized blame for her operation, the adhesions in her belly, the loss of viscera that caused her kidney to float and so on.

Later on, while we were still five, another challenging event occurred that changed my life. Our parents were arguing in the kitchen while my brother and I stood next to each other in the adjacent family room. As our parents fought, they began to escalate into violence, hitting each other. Faces were glowing red, arms were flailing, and hands were making slapping sounds as they landed on each other's faces. I could even perceive the energy emitting from their heads. Our mother started screaming, "Call

Uncle Tom! Call Uncle Tom!" Then our father exclaimed, "Don't you dare! Don't you dare! " My twin and I stood frozen in fear. We looked at each other searching for an answer as to what to do, trying to arrive at a sensible solution to a very scary situation. I was afraid our parents were going to kill each other, but if we called Uncle Tom, our father would be enraged; if we did not, our mother (or father) might be injured. Mom was 5'10" and weighed 165 lbs. where Dad weighed closer to 120 at the same height. The exchange appeared to me in slow motion, making it seem like it was taking forever to end. Apparently, as I learned later, my father had come home in the middle of the day in a drunken state, and my mother was furious with him. Finally, I nervously raced over to the phone and dialed the operator. This was in the days when phones had no dial or keypad and when you picked up the handset, the operator would respond, "Number, please." I did not know Uncle Tom's phone number. He and Aunt Henny, my mother's sister, lived very close by, and yet I barely knew their last name. We had been taught how to use the phone in an emergency, but we were unprepared for this. As the slow motion argument continued in the background, I eventually remembered and gave the operator their full name. She immediately connected us. Uncle Tom was a large man and could rescue my mother, if the situation came to that. I anxiously explained the situation to Aunt Henny and she sent Uncle Tom—which, in my five-year-old mind, also seemed to take forever. When he arrived, our mother and father quickly took their seats in the kitchen intending to appear as though nothing had happened. My brother and I stood in the family room with jaws dropped in shock when we heard them say they were just having "a discussion," and it was not necessary for him to investigate. I remember thinking that I could never trust my parents again. I decided I would take control of my own life from that point forward. Obviously I did not handle controlling my life very well.

I believe these events fueled my nightmares as they continued until my parents delivered the tree-top angel to my room later on when we were 8. After the decision to take control of my life at five years old, nightmares were no longer my most pressing concern. In the next few years, I would learn about abandonment, betrayal, and lewd behavior.

# 4 COMPLICATIONS

My brother and I started attending elementary school in September before turning 6 in early December. At least we were allowed to remain together in the same classroom. With the stressors at home, we needed to be together for support, even if unspoken and not knowing why. Twins are a psychic, emotional unit, and we felt that bond.

My brother and I often rode our bikes to the creek at the edge of our country town where it was still and quiet. I felt comforted being outdoors in the sunlight and loved to play with caterpillars and watch snails up close. In Japanese, they were called "chii sa na to mo da chi," or "little friends." I clearly remember as a little girl walking home from school on a warm, sunny summer day and I felt an immense sense of love. I felt in love with the whole world. A big, black carpenter ant caught my attention walking on the sidewalk. Love filled my entire being and extended out to that ant, and I wanted to show him. I picked him up to pet him and it only took a second for his pinschers to sink into my skin, tightly squeezing my finger. I was shocked. It hurt a lot and I tried to pull him off. When I pulled, his body came apart from his head and he still squeezed my finger. Along with physical pain I also suffered the sadness at having killed this ant when I just wanted to show love!  I finally got his pinschers off my finger and went on home. It was a precursor to the lesson that these critters need freedom to be who they are and I can love them from a short distance. I used to bring a caterpillar into the house, set it on the kitchen table and ask my mother to watch it for me while I went to the bathroom. She was not happy and told me to get it outside. I should have become an etymologist, but life took me in other directions. That experience was also a glimpse of what love felt like. I would have to grow considerably before I could hold that vibration.

It was the following summer our family attended the Methodist Church a few times, as well as the Baptist Church. Our parents were searching for a religious community for our family. Another argument ensued as we stopped on the sidewalk of Main Street in our town while walking home after a service. It seemed to be an all-or-nothing decision where the whole family had to attend one church or the other. Our mother won the battle, and we began attending the First Baptist Church where we learned we were born in sin and had to be saved. That image did not raise my flagging self-esteem at all.

After a few months, both parents decided to walk down the aisle to salvation. I was sitting near the front of the church as I watched my mother sobbing and shaking as she walked, and my father's facial expression was very somber. He committed to relinquishing alcohol and traded it in for rigid religious propaganda. My natural empathy for my mother reached a high pitch, and I began to sob, too. I could not bear to see her cry—it always tore me apart. I felt very alone as though they were going somewhere without me, so I decided to walk the aisle too, still crying. For some reason, I felt as though I had plunged straight into the darkness of hell rather than rejoicing in newfound salvation. But if I was going to be in hell, at least I would be there with my parents. Later on, I would realize this trauma was when my creative inner child left, split off, not to return for decades. She knew the oppression I was about to endure and took to safe haven.

During upcoming summers, my brother and I were sent to daily vacation Bible school as well as Baptist Church camp on a Lake Erie island. I remember watching the nightly showing of films about the lepers in Africa, with the insinuation that if we did not "get saved" and "behave like a Christian," we would contract the dreaded disease. One night during the showing of the film, I uncharacteristically rebelled and walked out, leaving the rest of the kids in the temple and embracing the beautiful outdoors on a star-filled, cool and refreshing night. That felt more like salvation to me than "salvation" did and was very liberating. I was surprised there were a lot of others milling about the grounds, and they had not contracted leprosy, perhaps I would be all right, too.

Eventually, after attending church three times a week for several years, I acquiesced into the entire dogma. My self-esteem plummeted among the arguments, over-control, suppression of creativity and spontaneity, and ridicule for being ugly at home, and the born-in-sin teachings at the church. And of course, my intuition was the devil talking to me. *That* was probably the most damaging doctrine of all. It cost me dearly—for decades. I do remember, though, I think around the age of 15 that I had decided to study my Bible and do daily devotions. I started reading and could not make head or tails of what was being said. I mentally asked, "How am I supposed to understand this?" I heard a reply from the unseen, "Intuition!" Right.

Our family did become very close with another family that attended the church. The father was the head deacon who had an obese wife, three daughters, and a delightfully comical son. We alternated every week having a meal after the Sunday evening service at each other's homes.

As my parents argued continuously (coincidentally, *especially* after the Sunday morning church service), I felt my father was being badgered by my mother. I adored him as a little girl, sitting next to him at meals, stroking his arm in adoration. The more they argued, the more I felt my father's depression and went to his emotional aid. I was "daddy's little girl," and my mother became increasingly jealous. On two occasions, she even packed her suitcases, yelling the entire time about her dissatisfaction with his and my relationship. After that, my father began to avoid and ignore me. He chose to hold onto my mother and abandon me. I felt crushed and became withdrawn. Later I would resist the truth that my father was an alcoholic. To make matters worse, it was about that time that our family doctor recommended to my mother that my twin brother and I be placed in separate classes at school. This was too much for me to bear. I was in a state of grief and loss.

As an affectionate little girl though, I gained much satisfaction from our family's weekly sharing of Sunday evening, post-service meals as we alternated locations with our church friends. The deacon-father had wavy, salt-and-pepper hair and was a large man, tall as well as robust. I innocently used to massage his back and play with his hair. He played with me on the floor like a father would. He became my substitute father, which made me feel very happy. The affection I felt for my birth father was transferred to this man. Finally, I felt loved.

By the time I was thirteen I was still terrified of our five-foot-ten mother. I was compliant and felt I had become her clone. My siblings' and my lives were severely restricted between the church's fear-based dogma and our mother's fear-driven control with rules that constantly shifted, forcing us to walk on eggs. I admired my beautiful, feisty older sister but could not follow her example and summon the courage to cross our mother. I was not allowed to choose my friends as ironically my mother felt no one was good enough. I could not even wear my socks the way I wanted. My mother would always adjust them. I would start my walk to school and when out of sight, change my socks back.

At this point, it did not take long for word to spread: my mother was having an affair with this man, the head deacon of our church. What a shock. My sister came home one day after having seen them together in town. She was seething with anger. I did not understand why she felt that way, but she was strong and stood up to our parents, so I reasoned she knew more than I. That was also the year I became a so-called "woman" with my first menses. My mother must have revealed this little tidbit of information to our deacon friend, my surrogate father. Shortly thereafter, when it was his family's turn to come to our house after the Sunday night service, my mother came into the living room where we were all talking and announced our snacks and sandwiches were ready in the kitchen. Our deacon friend told me to wait in the living room with him. I asked him why and he refused to answer. I trusted him implicitly, so I did not question further, though he had a strange look on his face. I thought something was wrong. There was, but nothing I had done.

When everyone had left the room, he pulled me to him around the corner and out of view, lifted me up off the floor and french-kissed me, my feet dangling about the height of his knees. I stared wide-eyed at him with his eyes closed, feeling shocked and having no clue what was going on. I felt as though my tongue was being sucked from its attachment, a painful, unpleasant experience. He was so presumptuous about it; and I was reeling in confusion. Having been disconnected from my intuition, I had no way to discern whether this action was right or wrong. I certainly had received no training about this subject. This was a little beyond instructions to not talk to strangers. In the fresh blossoming of my body with an already confusing accompaniment of adolescent chemistry, I submerged into an obsessive quandary over what had just happened.

His advances progressed into molestation, and I became more intensely bewildered wondering whether what was happening was right or wrong. I could not trust anyone as I had taken charge of my life when I was five and now I'm 13. It reminded me of my dreams of the man on the ladder at my four-year-old bedroom window. I often wonder if those dreams were precognitive, the man looked like this man, with the same lecherous look on his face. I could not ask my parents about it. My mother was already jealous because of my once close relationship with my father. If she knew the man with whom she was having an affair was paying attention to me, she would probably disown me. If I asked my father about it, he would most likely have a stroke, or want to kill one of them. I kept quiet and withdrew even deeper. Here I went, deeper into hell and darkness.

Finally, my feelings led me to an answer. I became more disappointed and depressed over the betrayal of this man and his lusty motives. I believe he was working toward a rape. I developed a strong hatred for him—and for my mother. I brazenly refused any longer to have anything to do with him or his family, and he became angry with me for refusing his advances. He would make his way to me after church services and as though engaging in the customary hand-shakes, would hold my hand while quoting poetry like he was in love with me. I was repulsed. When he lead the Wednesday night prayer meetings at the church, he would insidiously offer prayers meant for me due to my refusal to be "close" with him. I was disgusted. My hatred for him grew stronger, and I grieved another loss and betrayal. I needed love and affection, but that was not it.

One Saturday after I disconnected from the deacon and his family, I went to my girlfriend's house in the country to play and ride her pony. She went to the same church, and we were in school together. I was feeling self-destructive at this point and refused to use a bridal, halter, or saddle on the pony. I actually and with awareness told myself I wanted to break my arm to get attention at home. I nudged the pony's sides to signal him to canter. But then he turned unexpectedly, and I did not. I fell over the pony's side, landing on the ground and jamming my right upper arm. My girlfriend was trained in first aid and ran into the house to retrieve a sling she had made for her course. (She trained and worked as a nurse as an adult.) She placed it on my arm while her father called my parents to pick me up. She thought my arm might be broken. The x-ray at the doctor's office confirmed her suspicion, there was a fracture, but it had been immobilized by the sling my friend skillfully applied, and I did not require a cast. She was a heroine.

And my strategy worked. My mother felt sorry for me, having my monthly moon-time and a broken arm simultaneously was more than any thirteen-year-old needed. She sat on the couch with her arm around me-- once. That was it. I felt victimized and lonely. If only—if only I could have recognized that the power of my mind to visualize and create a broken arm to get attention was the same power I could harness to create a happy life. I might have been able to make better decisions and utilize my personal power. That awareness would come much further down the road.

# 5 SMALL STEPS TO PROGRESS – TWO FORWARD, ONE BACK

The remainder of my teenage years was spent mostly hiding in shyness with an inability to communicate with people. I loved my twin brother and our miniature Dachshund. They were my only connections to Light during those dark years. Playing flute in the high school band was a seed of discipline that would serve me in adulthood and in retrospect, music was some salvation. I sang in the choir and special groups as well as at our church. But I still had frequent thoughts of suicide or running away, having the courage for neither. There was simply nowhere to go and I could trust no one. Sometimes I became so enraged at my mother, being unable to communicate my feelings, I would beat myself in the stomach with my fists. According to her, I could not do anything right, and my low self-esteem was reinforced when she told me I "looked dead." I just wanted to escape. Indeed, my face was pale as her projections onto me, energetic assaults, drained my life force. Later, I would thank God for make-up and always made sure I wore plenty of rouge or blush to compensate for my pale countenance. Perhaps my "looking dead" was merely a manifestation of my yearning to escape or die or the impact of the treatment I was receiving at home.

Sometimes I would look at the shape of my body and recognize it was shaped just like my mother's. I considered her to be fat and assumed that opinion for my own body. I detested when wearing shorts I would sit down and see my thighs spread out, a natural result, but lacking muscle tone or definition, I felt repulsed. But photographs from those days reveal the truth of my physique. I was very thin and gangly and looked as delicate as I felt. Like a wisp, a delicate flower. It wasn't that my mother was fat either,

15

though she was 5' 10" and weighed 165 pounds. (Our family doctor tagged me "the little one" in comparison to my sister and mother.) We both lacked muscle tone and strength as a result of ignorance about and absence of physical exercise. (I wanted to join the high school cheerleaders at one point, but was socially withdrawn, and the impetus it would take to audition was stifled by fear.) I was sickly from using my lunch money to buy chocolate and candy from the gas station I passed on the way to school. Sugar was my drug of choice and only served to further weaken my physical condition. It numbed my emotions too so that I didn't slip and allow the rage building within me to discharge, bringing slaps in the face from my mother, accompanied by more yelling so painful to my ears and harsh to my delicate psyche. In physical education class, I couldn't even run across the gym floor without becoming severely out of breath. The lack of proper nutrition showed up in my check-ups at the doctor's office. It was official: I had the liver of an old person and was anemic. The doctor gave me a liquid supplement containing iron that left a constant after taste of metal, like I had a spoon in my mouth, and caused me to gain weight. Soon I felt the heavy feeling of extra weight and stopped by my own choice, with increased hatred for my body. My mother hated cooking and used lifeless canned foods and turned burgers into rocks. I felt there should be a pill people could take instead of eating. My addiction to sugar was to be a problem well into my adult years.

My twin brother was badgered and beaten by our parents because his grades were lower than mine. This treatment of him brought great sadness to me, so I unconsciously offered him sisterly protection by bringing my own grades down to narrow the chasm between them. As a young adult, I had a dream that was greatly impactful and I didn't understand what it meant until I consulted with a friend that taught intuition classes in corporations and knew dream interpretation. The dream started out with me sitting on a couch in a living room across from a man also on a couch. I was speaking to the man in fluent Spanish, which I do not speak in the waking state. I looked over to my right where there was a wall with a tapestry hanging. My consciousness zoomed into the tapestry and I was immediately transported to a field or pasture. I was a little boy and there was a little donkey standing next to me. I adored this donkey. I looked out into the expanse of the sky and saw a huge, dangerous-looking storm approaching and knew I had to take my donkey into protection. There was a hole in the ground and I tried to push my donkey into the hole so he would be out of harm's way. He refused. Time and again with the storm quickly approaching, I worked to get him into the hole for protection. He still refused and pushed me into the hole. He laid down on his right side to cover the hole. The storm hit. It was massive and destructive. When the storm passed, I crawled up out of the hole. My beloved donkey was lying still on his right side and there was a spear piercing his left side. He was dead. I cried so hard in the dream that I woke myself up. I was crying in the waking state as well. I was deeply saddened and feeling tremendous grief at this loss.

My friend asked me when I inquired about the dream's meaning if I had a twin. I answered him in the affirmative and he proceeded with the interpretation. He said the donkey represents intelligence, they are highly intelligent creatures and this fact was recognized by my dreamer self. The spear in the left side of the donkey represented my left brain, my intellectual side and it was "killed" through the destruction of the storm, representing our parents. I grieved the loss of my intellect, sacrificed for the sake of my twin brother in protection against our stormy parents.

The "killing" of my intellect was a gift for my brother so he didn't have to endure so much violence against him over school grades and it provided a seed of power for me since I couldn't protect myself, I at least could provide more ease for him.

My dear brother had to deal with bullies at school -- as well as at home. Then after high school, came Viet Nam and Agent Orange--hence diabetes--and post-traumatic stress disorder.

The dysfunction in our family, the constant arguing and yelling, and the necessity to walk on eggshells, affected our ability to study and comprehend. I remember when the school guidance counselor called me in to his office and commented that my test scores indicated I was capable of much higher grades. He asked if anything was wrong. Wrong? I did not know anything was wrong; I thought everyone lived the way we were. I enjoyed learning but was emotionally exhausted from constantly walking on eggshells at home that eventually conditioned me into a constant state of hyper vigilance. The ritual spankings by our mother had stopped but were replaced by sudden angry outbursts ending with a slap to my face. If I communicated in a way that revealed my own anger or any sense of power, I received a slap. Not only did those slaps quiet my tongue, they encouraged me to deny and suppress *any* angry expression—or even expression of any desire—a costly lesson. The slaps eventually stopped, too, as my mother's handprint would remain on my face long after as a telltale sign. (Perhaps my delicacy served me in this instance.) She was concerned what people might think if they saw her handprint on my face. Then we were just down to the screaming in my face over my failure to meet the requirements of the constantly changing and arbitrary household rules. I never measured up in any category. Both my mother and my sister made fun of the way I fixed my hair and my hand-me-down clothes. Sometimes I felt like Cinderella as they would go shopping together and I stayed at home. I would sit on the heat register and cry to our Doxie how nobody loved me. I had mastered powerlessness.

As far as friends, I did have a neighbor friend that was slightly younger than I. In eighth grade, I had begun lessons and then was prematurely thrust into the high school band in ninth, but it was a great foundation towards learning a discipline. My friend and I sat near each other in the flute section and would get together to practice, especially since we also both went to the same church. We eventually played flute duets during the services. I would feel sad though when we would make a date to get together and she would call and cancel at the last minute because her wealthy neighbor invited her to swim in her backyard pool. I felt I was not good enough to be invited and self-esteem remained elusive. I was in such an unconscious state that it was almost like being drunk and "out of it." I was a loner for the most part.

When I was fifteen, however, a clue as to part of my perceptual gifts emerged in a family scenario. When I read a magazine article on mental health disorders like neuroses, psychoses and schizophrenia, I was captivated. As I devoured the information about neuroses, I immediately recognized my father's behavior. Walking enthusiastically from the living room to where my parents were sitting at the kitchen table one Saturday morning, my father staring into space in a depressed daze, I announced "Hey Dad! You're neurotic! " He came slightly out of his trance with a quizzical expression on his face, "Huh? Whaat...?" I repeated, "You're a neurotic! " My mother shushed me and sent me scurrying out of the room. My father returned to his blank stare. He was so depressed. Later that day, my mother revealed that my father had just returned from an appointment with a psychiatrist—and had received the diagnosis of neuroses. The incident was a hint as to my interest in psychology and my ability to recognize behavior patterns that would be remembered and awakened at a later time. I even asked my mother if I could see a psychiatrist to discuss my own anxiousness, but she said no for fear of being judged a "bad mother." I submerged back into a deep hypnotic stupor, like father, like daughter. I would eventually block my memories from my awareness to avoid the feelings so in need of recognition. That recognition would have to come much later. I escaped from the world and my reality in the healing plane of sleep. I already was having suicidal thoughts and would cowardly sidestep the issue by merely cutting myself shaving. I continued on, going through the motions of living, until I became attracted to a fellow.

# I Forgive You, Daddy – Yoga and the Angels Healed Me!

I was smitten by one of the guys in my high school class. Tall and thin, blonde and handsome with a beautiful smile, he belonged to the same denomination of church and we both sang in the high school and church choirs. We began dating a little in high school, he played football and I played flute. We sang a couple of duets at church and I was in total infatuation with him. (I do not believe I was capable of real love yet as emotionally immature as I was.) It was typical swoon-style love. We continued to see each other until he went to college out of state and I stayed at home in our tiny town and went to business school. We went out when he came home on breaks and during holidays.

I was grateful to my parents for paying for executive secretary training at a nearby business school so I could obtain suitable employment. I wanted to go to college to become an English teacher, but was terrified. The application asked questions that required some savvy to answer. With no mentor, and feeling embarrassed at my inability to determine the answers myself, I procrastinated until it was too late to apply. Besides, it was an application to a religious college and I was puzzled about that. A representative of the business school in the next town seemed to magically appear, stopping by our house one evening to see if I wanted to attend. It seemed like an answer to an unspoken prayer, a subconscious hope. The Universe was taking care of me. My parents enrolled me in the 12-month course that would build on the typing class I took in high school. With a major in music, English and languages, office professional training seemed alien. I did not study or do well in the beginning; it is difficult to function in a state of unconsciousness. Somehow a fellow and I connected at the school and we decided to car pool. He picked me up on his way from where I still lived with my parents and drove us to the business school. I remember singing with the music on the radio and he once asked if I meant the words of the songs for him. Rather an odd question I thought. Where did he get that idea?

I remember one professor, a co-owner of the business school who shared teaching most of the classes with his wife. He called on me to answer a question in a business law class. I had not studied and blushed with embarrassment when I tried to fake my way through an answer. He was not at all kind about it. My grades reflected my poor attitude in a status report to my parents and they lectured me about the cost. If I was not going to put forth the effort to learn the material, they threatened to pull me from the course. I fearfully woke up sufficiently to embrace the education and eventually made the Dean's List. I did appreciate my parents' efforts and graduated with reputation intact.

The fellow that drove me to the business school had fallen in love with me, unbeknownst to me. I was totally unaware of his feelings (as I was unaware of most things then) until he one day proposed marriage. I was shocked. During the course of the school year, he had been ill with an infection in the lining of his heart causing him to miss a lot of school, and I went to see him in an attempt to uplift his spirits. We did a few things together, like going for a ride on his motorcycle, but I was oblivious to any romantic leanings. That is how engrossed I was in my own little world until many years later. I felt like I broke his heart and when he did find a partner, she looked at me with disdain like I did something horrible. In adult life, I called him to apologize for my inconsiderateness.

My beloved blonde boyfriend came home from college and he also proposed. At age 19, we became engaged. He bought a beautiful marquis diamond that I was proud to wear.

Then somewhere along the line, I determined I had to break off the engagement. When he was home on break, we sat in his little Nash Rambler in the cold of winter parked in the spot relegated to the Rambler next to the barn on their farm. I did most of the talking. He mimicked caring as though he wanted to stay together, but deep inside, nearly unconsciously, I did not believe it. I convinced him we should break up and returned his ring, which was eventually passed on to his mother. I was heartbroken and became depressed. Why did I break it off? My mother did not believe he truly cared for me, was her dominant influence so great I would take this action? Are we capable at age 19 of responsible love? I began to sleep even more—after work and before dinner, Saturday mornings, naps on Sunday afternoons—12 hours a day. Depression deepened and life became even darker.

Once I graduated from the 12-month course in executive office training directly after high school, I landed a job working as secretary to the manager of a medical clinic while living with my parents where I stayed for a few years. (I graduated from high school at age 17 since my birthday fell late in the year). I waited until I was 18 to get my driver's license since my brother and sister were already arguing with our parents over borrowing their car. I bought my brother's first used Ford before I even had my license. It sat on a cement slab next to our garage for a year or so until I had my license and freedom to drive as needed. Eventually I moved into my first apartment, around the age of 21. It seemed strange and wonderful to be alone but the sounds of the family arguments and the assaults on my ears whenever I was caught "not doing anything right" continued in my head for years. I kept my place clean as those were my perfectionist days and I withdrew into deeper isolation, feeling intensely sad, not knowing why. I always felt a jittery sense of anxiety, ever since I can remember after that first dream at 4 years old. My parents drove to the same city I lived in where my sister was on the farther side of the same town. They visited her and her family with 3 sons, but they never stopped to see me. I descended deeper into the feelings of being the victim. I tried desperately to win their approval, but failed just as desperately.

After buying my brother's car, the first major purchase I made was a beautiful horse. I had wanted a pony as a child and since it was neither practical or affordable for my parents, I waited until I could buy one myself. I boarded him at a friend's farm, but nearly always rode alone. He was a wonderful, 4-year-old Bay gelding that could neck reign easily with the training he had already received. He trained me to ride and in the ways of Horse. My empathy and intuition of which I was not even aware yet helped us to bond and I could follow his leads, in addition to a few hints from friends. I remember the first time I put his bridle on by myself, I got it backwards and he stood there patiently while I figured it out. I loved the country and we went often through fields and over country roads and best of all to the fairgrounds which was a wide open area where we could run. My horse (Cochise was his name when I bought him, I didn't want to confuse him by changing it) would run gleefully and I would feel a blip of his hind quarters lifting a little. He was bucking in a full gallop, kicking up his heels at the joy of running freely! My own feeling of freedom with his mane waving and the wind blowing across my face as I hunched down close to him was magical. My only concern was if there were a hole in the ground and he tripped in it, but that never happened. Sometimes I would ride him into town near my parents' house and let other people ride him while I held the reigns. He did not like red vehicles, so I was watchful. He would shy away and prance princely past them as though the vehicle would jump out at him. We always got through it, unscathed. He was a bright spot in my life and was warm in winter when I rode him bareback.

I kept myself insulated in the days leading up to my attempt, but after changing jobs to earn more income, I met a man there that was very kind to me. We worked in the same office of the steel plant, which around 1968 was a booming business. I did not stay at that job long as the soot from the blast furnaces floated everywhere and constantly having to breathe it in, I endured 5 sinus infections in one winter. I moved on to an office job close to my apartment, and remained in contact with my friend. We began to go out together.

In the relationship, now around age 22, I discovered that I had no communication or decision making skills. He would take me out to eat and I had no idea what I wanted to order. It seems strange now, to be so timid and indecisive that I was unable to choose a meal from a menu. My wants were drummed out of me by my over-controlling mother years before. I remember deciding to give up wanting because I could never have what I wanted—a life-changing decision. Anything I wanted was denied, anything I was promised never materialized—it almost seemed like conspiracy.

As my friend and I dated more frequently I convinced myself I loved him, the truth is I was "in need" with him. Most of the time, I just wanted to be held and he provided that kind of closeness. I felt like I was purring just with his arm around me. This friend is the one that helped me when I was too depressed to stop crying and go out to get something to eat.

I was living alone in my apartment in a town about a half hour away from where I grew up. I worked in the office a short drive away. This was when I became even more deeply depressed and began taking the tranquilizers more regularly. I had told my family doctor that I was "just like my mother" when I requested them. My mother gave them to me when I would get nervous before a band concert, so I figured I needed them now. I didn't really understand what they did for me, I continued to feel anxious.

Then one day in May 1970, at age 23, I sat down on my bed with the bottle in my hands preparing to take my usual dosage. I began to wonder what miracle was supposed to be hiding in these little green and black capsules. I decided to stop taking them to see who I was without them—I obviously had not arrived in Shangri-La while taking them, so I put the bottle away and on my way I went.

By October, I was so depressed I could hardly eat. My friend brought me food from McDonald's because I was crying so much I wouldn't go out to buy groceries. I felt totally alone. It was as though everyone else in the world was happy except me, and there was some secret or joke to which I was not privy. I returned to the medicine cabinet and retrieved the bottle of Librium. Shaking out a palm full of the capsules, I held them in one hand as I poured the Vodka into a Tupperware tumbler until it was three-quarters full. (Where did that come from? I didn't normally drink.) I took the pills with the Vodka—which was supposed to be tasteless, but was disgusting. Again, on my way I went, forgetting about my decision to end my misery.

Later the same day, I was walking across the living room of my apartment and remembered my decision. How could I still be alive after ingesting all those pills? I was not even sleepy! I was surprised at this turn of events... and then... I heard a voice booming out of nowhere: "Now,

Michelle, you must clean up your life." I wondered what in the world that meant.

Still crying frequently and not eating much, and after repeatedly pressing me, I finally was convinced by my friend that I should seek counseling. I felt as terrified at the prospect of that as I did by my childhood nightmares. I was certain my mother had gone before me to the counselor and told him what a horrible person I was and as a result was doomed to live in someone's prison of domination. When I arrived at the counselor's office, I sobbed so intensely I could barely utter my name. He admitted me to the hospital for a couple of days, and the rest from the stresses of my life and job felt wonderful. As a teenager, sometimes after a nap (sleeping as another avenue of escape) my face would glow. It was visible to others as well as me. Throughout my childhood, I noticed what amazing powers of recuperation I possessed, and this hospital stay was no exception. Even my doctor was surprised at my quick, but ultimately superficial, recovery. When he discharged me that second day, he told me to "go get interested in something I liked." So I did.

When I was little, perhaps 5 or 6, my parents had a calendar hanging in the upstairs hallway. Each month had a different photograph of an utterly beautiful ballerina, sometimes with her danseur, statuesque in some graceful fairy flight *en pointe*. I loved the ballerina's long and thin, sculpted legs, fine, like deer and remember standing so small beneath the calendar and looking up at the images held in an eternal dancer's pose. These images tapped on the shoulder of my muse and plucked the strings of my appreciation for beauty. I had taken a year of lessons at the local library during junior high, but the instructor moved on since only two of us in the entire school were interested in ballet. Now at age of 23, I decided to start dance lessons at the local studio fulfilling my counselor's command to get involved in something that inspired me. I began with a half hour Saturday morning ballet class and loved it in spite of having to push through my introverted nervousness. I was already slender, but my body was weak and board-like, stiff from years of abusing it with high intakes of sugar and lack of nutritious food. Within a short time, I was awarded a scholarship for six months, meaning I could take all the dance classes I wanted for free, as long as I kept paying for my Saturday morning ballet class. My one instructor (the mother part of a mother-daughter team) was very pushy, which is exactly what I needed since I was painfully shy and inhibited. The Universe was taking care of me again—in spite of myself. It was the start of my physical healing, strengthening, and developing more discipline. My instructor told me that even when I was feeling poorly, I should still come to class. She claimed I would always feel better afterward; she was right.

Both instructors beckoned me to join them in a Yoga class on the upper floor of the studio where we normally practiced gymnastics. I was suspicious of the class, having grown up in a small mid-western town and never having heard of Yoga. Whenever they tried to explain what it was, it never made sense to me. Eventually, I acquiesced and tagged along. It was like putting on an old shoe. At first it was a little strange, but as I began to relax, it was very natural. I was hooked. I have been immersed ever since.

The Yoga teacher at the studio sometimes referred nonchalantly to past lives and telepathic communication with her husband, which was frightening to me. I stopped going to class temporarily out of fear but soon returned because otherwise it felt good. It seemed like a new concept in my life, relaxing and feeling *good*. Once I learned more about it through study in the coming years, I felt the unseen was totally natural. I persisted and practiced Yoga for hours at a time, sometimes rising between 3:30 and 5:00 a.m. to fit it in before going to work, practicing more on weekends, and I began meditating. It was the only peace of mind—actually with glimpses of the *promise* of peace, in the initial stages—that I had ever found. I had prayed for many years, but that was more like begging God or Jesus to bring me relief from emotional pain and the noise from years of family arguments reverberating relentlessly in my head, or to save me from lecherous men and energy vampires. At times, I pondered how I could feel so peaceful in that meditative state when I felt so fractured in my waking journey, though at the time I could not articulate what I was feeling since I had never experienced wholeness. The dissonance was such a wide crevasse, how would I ever build a bridge to understanding? Who had this information? All would unfold as I walked this journey.

Meditation was different from prayer. After practicing Yoga postures and upon entering meditation, often emotions would surface from some unknown storehouse, and I would weep with deep sadness at the loss of something I could not articulate even to myself, let alone a counselor. Slowly, my meditations filled more with pleasant spiritual experiences than the surging emotional releases. But the chasm between my inner and outer life remained irreconcilable for decades to come. How could everything be wonderful inside and so chaotic outside? For years I could not understand that dichotomy. Eventually healing and answers would come.

I attended Yoga classes with various local teachers for 15 years before beginning my own teaching career. During that time, some of my teachers tried to encourage me to teach, but I was terrified of the responsibility. Eventually though I felt a "calling" to teach and did for another 10 years, when I felt guided to enroll in a teacher training program and became certified through Kripalu. I opened to deeper, more intense healing as I continued the path with training in Yoga therapy, Yoga dance, Reiki and other healing modalities.

What I am about to share are accounts about the meditation and spiritual aspects of Yoga and some of my healing and psychic experiences during my journey back to Wholeness. Many people all over the world have had these types of experiences, they are not necessarily unique, though some are unusual and very interesting. My purpose for expressing them is to help expand your awareness that these methods (Yoga, meditation, Reiki, as well as astrology, psychic perceptions, channeling, telepathy, so-called past-life recall, Angels and other consciousness study methods and teachers in the unseen worlds) offer valid benefits, which may bring hope to you and others. Also, I have come to believe that the physical body holds our memories in our cells until we are ready to remember, experience, and heal the issues. If I had learned Yoga and meditation when I was young and troubled by nightmares, fears, feeling powerless and terrorized by Life itself, I doubt I would have experienced many of the trials I endured before Wholeness was restored. Those trials, however, caused me to reach deep into the Universal Blueprint for Immense Strength and Courage and pull it to me, anchoring it within my own depths. And the capacity for understanding the plight of others, inspiring a desire to be of service, are all pieces of the puzzle in the quilted fabric of my destiny.

After the attempt, my friend and I continued seeing each other. I had already convinced myself I loved him out of the fear of being alone and after several years, we married. He was very kind and generous with me so it was easy to confuse my dependency on him for partnership love. He was more like a father to me actually. While we were married, he encouraged me to go back to college. His encouragement was more like the feeling of "not good enough" without a college degree, but I went. My whole world opened up through the college experience. I started out slowly with 2 courses and built up to full time. But our relationship could not bear the fast rate of expansion I was experiencing and my newfound independence. I would later graduate from community college with a major in physical education, but 2 quarters before graduation, I left him abruptly, still unable to communicate very well and possessing little self-assertion. Avoidance was my *modus operandi* for the time and it had to suffice. But I could not tolerate his dominance and directing me where I did not want to go. His demands upon me to be a "wife" with all the accompanying duties (cooking, cleaning, all the things his mother was great at), were too much pressure when I was growing in another direction. I simply was not good "wife" material to fill his needs. He wanted me to cut back on my precious dance classes and he despised my dance teachers. All he did when I was home was read his law journals or the newspaper and I needed movement and stimulation at that time. I needed to grow without someone dominating me, in spite of lingering immaturity. Once I moved out, I lived with a roommate for a while so I could gather myself together and make some decisions.

After I finished those last two quarters, I graduated from college with honors and took a higher paying job in downtown Cleveland as a legal assistant. Working in the city in the legal field was stressful so on Fridays after work I would stop for a glass of wine with a co-worker. I was nervous even around her, she was beautiful and confident. I, on the other hand, could hardly make eye contact with anybody. But one glass of wine on an empty stomach gave me false courage and after a few short moments of comforting numbness, a deep sadness would wash over me, emotions clambering for recognition that bubbled up to the surface of my consciousness. I never stayed long at the restaurant. I was constantly looking for approval – from anyone – and was terrified to socialize. Sadness erupted through a flood of tears as I drove home.

One Friday evening, my boss' married friend stuck around the upscale bar and when I left, he followed me home. I was once again drunk on one glass of wine, and he pretended to be concerned for my welfare on the road. After a little wine, immense sadness again surfaced, and I sobbed as I drove down the expressway, still not knowing why. He followed me up to my apartment and into my bedroom under the false pretense of caring. In the morning, my new black dress I had worn to work the day before was in a heap on my bedroom floor. As he told me that night how he wanted me, I slipped, still crying, into unconsciousness at which time he slipped himself into me. That next morning I was physically sore and was infuriated with him. For once I expressed my contempt for someone's lack of integrity, compassion or even decency. He was gone but had left his gloves at my place and when he came to pick them up the next day, I told him how I felt about what he had done. That was the last time I drank anything containing alcohol. I did not need to follow in my father's footsteps. Even though he stopped drinking when I was six, my father's behavior patterns and the family's dysfunction caused sufficient impact to remind me that alcohol could be treacherous, at least for me.

I continued attending classes in dance and Yoga and practiced consistently at home. Dance brought to me a sense of belonging, albeit distantly, to a new community, and Yoga fit well into my isolated existence. I began to jog and was physically active, playing racquetball with a co-worker and going biking. I began to feel better. After leaving my counselor's care before he thought I was ready, it was time to go back and let him know how well I was doing.

As I entered the front door to his reception room, I saw him talking with a departing client. Then...the feeling of slow motion began again...I looked over at my counselor across the room...his client just having left...I saw a dingy yellow, wobbling, bubble of energy coming from his solar plexus region...directly toward me. When it hit me, I regressed into the powerless, young girl who was in trouble and came to see him... I felt the depression and fear all over again. When I followed him into his office, my sense of time returned to normal. I tried to explain how well I was doing, but the feeling of gloom had gripped me, and I could not regain the enthusiasm that brought me to see him. I stared at my feet just like I always did before. I subsequently learned through my studies of psychicism and energy that the bubble of energy was his fear, and that I had a clairvoyant experience. But I absorbed his fear (the yellow energy ball) and was not strong enough to hold my new enthusiasm for life. I think he preferred me ill. Who was I to discharge myself from his care, even though I knew I was not ready? I experienced a breakdown in trust with him as he sided with my husband over some issues and that was enough for me.

In light of all my newfound Yoga and meditation techniques, and in spite of the breakdown in trust with him, I sent my counselor letters describing some of my experiences. Still living mostly in isolation, I had no one with whom to share my feelings and experiences; in desperation, I tried to maintain a communication connection with my counselor which served a purpose more like journaling, still quite effective. One of the techniques I learned in my studies was to relax into stillness and imagine going to a cave where a Wise Old Sage would be waiting. The Sage would answer questions and offer advice regarding my life and decisions. I pretended that my counselor was the Sage and asked him many questions during meditation. The answers that I received seemed to help; certainly the relaxation did, and I was visual enough to have good experiences. But I did not yet have the knowledge of how to handle someone else's fear energy–I was still learning to handle my own. Apparently, my meditative success bumped up against some of his insecurities or maligned with his belief systems. I thought he would be proud of my self-sufficiency in finding my own answers. His "yellow bubble of fear" was a sure sign of his disbelief around my new techniques. However, his receptionist/assistant told me how much she enjoyed reading my experiences before she filed them in the cabinet. It may seem like a violation of privacy for her to read my letters, but she was his assistant and I was just glad *someone* was reading them and getting *something* from them. She reminded me of Della in the Perry Mason series.

Many years later, when I was around 35 and had practiced a lot more

Yoga, I would have another spiritual experience worthy of note. Upon moving to a suburb of Cleveland, I joined a running club that met across the street from my apartment. I had been running alone for about 10 years—it was nice to connect with other people; we ran in the Metro parks which also afforded us the opportunity to connect with Nature. It took me at least the previous six years of Yoga and meditation to quiet my family's voices I heard arguing and screaming in my head. I mostly remained a hermit and used the time for study and for healing my soul. After running several miles, I would come home, stretch and practice Yoga. I used to weep when working with hip openers and butterfly stretches. I did not know specifically from where the sadness originated, but I allowed myself to release through tears. I increased my fitness routine with jogging and eventually increased to fifteen miles, running for two hours on the bike path in the Metro parks where Nature assisted in my healing. A fellow running companion from the club mentioned an anger management group in one of our conversations. He had attended the group himself and felt it was helping him become aware of and release anger. I inquired about it thinking the group might allow me to explore some of my deeper feelings that were emerging during Yoga practice.

During one of the few group sessions in which I participated, the facilitator asked me why I had such a sad look on my face all the time. I began to feel hot and embarrassed, yet it seemed he was onto something. I could not answer, and he persisted in prying me open. I began to cry, and I shook from a place deep within me. The atmosphere in the room changed into a golden glow. The very air was a thick gold color and I felt somewhat like I was in another place, like a different dimension. Part of me recognized that I was accessing a deep-seated issue, but part of me was terrified. Others in the group begged the facilitator to leave me alone, could he not see I was extremely upset? I continued to cry, feeling the heat in my body rise and my face became red. My glasses steamed up, and my ears were hot. He kept pressing me for an answer. The room was still filled with that golden energy when I finally dislodged a piece of understanding from deep within me.

I looked sad all the time because... because... ... I THOUGHT IT MIGHT CAUSE SOMEONE TO CARE. There. I said it. Some of the others in the group were *appalled* at the facilitator for causing me to be so upset, but he felt he knew what he was doing. His strategy worked, though his refusal to let me off the hook was perhaps a little harsh. It felt good to be able to come up with an answer myself, instead of being told what to think. I believe I made some new connections in my brain with that incident. After another meeting or two with him, he revealed he wanted me to help my running friend that referred me with his process. I could hardly believe my ears that he wanted me to stay in a relationship with this man, just so I could help him heal. This guy was married! It was a mistake to become involved with him in the first place. Here was another breakdown in trust with a therapist. I was paying for my own counseling, not there to adhere to the whims of the counselor that seemed to care more about this fellow than me. I left that group and I broke off the relationship with my runner friend. My newly blossoming sense of Guidance was leading me to depend on myself for my own healing rather than seeking counseling from other Humans. That is one of the smartest decisions I ever made.

# 6 THE ONSET OF PEACE, BEAUTY AND THE UNUSUAL

After those few sessions in the anger management support group, I felt I had gained what I needed and decided to move on. I learned that my mother, father, sister, and brother, as well as myself, were all doing the best we could at any given time. I had spent time beating pillows, talking with an image of one of them in an empty chair to "hear" their side of the story, and gained great insight and understanding to release anger. Through my Yoga study and practice, I also found that I could merely become aware of the stifled emotion, be with it (experience it), and then let it pass through me as effectively as beating pillows, and without any drama. Yoga brought me to a place where I could accept and experience the emotion then release it rather than acting out, sending it out into the Universe for it to return to me manifest in some scenario. My life was beginning to head in a more peaceful direction, and became *very* interesting.

As I look back, even some early events let me know that my life would be quite unusual. While I was still working as an office professional for the manager at the medical clinic, I underwent somewhat of an Awakening. I was 19 or 20 then, so the year would have been around 1966. My sister and her husband invited me to see their new apartment in a nearby small town and perhaps to celebrate over coffee. After a tour of her new apartment and chatting for a few minutes, my sister and I decided to explore the area to find a coffee shop. We traveled probably half an hour beyond her home towards Akron (Ohio). It was an early fall evening so the last indigo hues of dusk gave way to the velvety black night. The city lights projected their radiance upward dissipating into the clear, dark sky, muting all but the brightest stars. Meandering in unfamiliar territory, we were nearly lost but knew which of the state highways would bring us back. It appeared we were in the industrial section of Akron, judging from the mostly one-story, warehouse-type buildings with fenced-in gravel parking lots.

I was driving, and as I happened to look up through the windshield toward the sky, there was a huge, beautifully lit, soundless, soaring object. It was circular with a smooth, slightly rounded dome top and windows lining the edge. I estimated it was hovering at around 1,000 feet. Someone must have been occupying it because it was brightly lit up--and moving. The windows were aglow, although I didn't see anyone inside, and there was a floodlight-type beam emanating from the center underneath, much like a landing light. I was awestruck and intrigued. The entire object was a cement-beige color, and it was absolutely silent. The windows had divisions looking very much like traditional human windows as I watched it hover and spin in very slow, circular revolutions. The floodlight poured a column of light over the buildings below, and I wanted to stop the car to watch more easily--but we were in the midst of traffic. Why was not the whole city at a standstill watching this marvel? I personally was captivated. Finally, I found a parking lot behind a warehouse, pulled in, and parked the car. My sister was very quiet, just staring ahead. She apparently did not share my excitement and made no comment. I opened my car door and stood on the floorboard so I could get a better view--what a fantastic sight. The craft was silently sailing, as though whoever was inside was out for a Sunday drive; I wondered if they were merely observing the city preparing for its nightly repose.

As my sister sat apparently mesmerized in the car, I returned to the driver's seat. She was staring straight ahead through the windshield as I got in--but the craft was in the sky, up and to her right!  She was not even looking at it.  And she never spoke a word. As I watched, the craft turned off the lights glowing through the windows, and then the floodlight went dark. The next thing I remember is it had disappeared. I got the impression the occupants became aware they were being observed and decided to leave. I questioned my sister about seeing it, and she confirmed she had. We called our parents immediately to tell them about this incident, since we figured no one would believe us if we hesitated. We did not have to look far to locate a pay phone, and we reassured our mother, who seemed to be taking all this in stride, that we had not been imbibing, indeed, the coffee shop remained elusive. Interestingly, a friend of mine said she heard a report of this sighting on the radio the next day, but I did not hear the report personally.

Having been raised in a strict fundamental church, this sighting was a highly significant occurrence. The appearance of the flying object served to further put a wrench in the religious works--at least for me. As a child I always had questions and unresolved issues around some of the teachings I received, none of which were answered to my satisfaction. One serious concern was this: if people had to be "saved" by Jesus in order to gain entry to Heaven, what about the people who lived for thousands of years before He arrived? Were they all doomed to hell when they died? And--our preachers certainly never mentioned extra-terrestrials or UFOs in their sermons. What would be the ramifications of other-worldly creatures that have not been "saved" by Jesus? Perhaps God is a little bigger than manmade religion gives credit. As a child watching Japanese black and white movies of aliens landing on the Earth, I intuitively knew that extra-terrestrials existed, and I had no doubt in that--no doubt whatsoever. My sister and I never did locate the local coffee shop--but who cared, stumbling onto this find was mega-more exciting. She never initiated conversation about it, though she did mention it to her three sons. I kept checking in with her to see if she blocked the memory from her mind. She always confirmed that we saw this object together.

At work the next day, I enthusiastically described my experience and was greatly discouraged to find there were those who not only refused to believe extra-terrestrials existed, but they did not believe me, an honest person. I must admit that I, at age 19 or 20 and still reeling from growing up in my dysfunctional family, was already considered "spacey." But my youthful exuberance was deflated. I do believe this experience was merely a hint at what was in store for me in another couple of decades.

In my mid-thirties, I continued practicing Yoga and meditation, my inner life was becoming rich and colorful. I was attending an hour and a half Yoga class once or twice a week during this time, the early 1980's, and practicing frequently at home. Arriving home after class, I would meditate with a candle for an hour or so. While focusing on the candle flame initially with my eyes open, I relaxed and then closed my eyes. The flame would appear as an imprint on my mind's eye, and I focused on it, developing concentration and depth. After a while, I gradually became aware that the flame in my mind's eye had changed. I felt as though I had been far away or very deep within for a few moments—an experience of profound stillness and wellbeing--and was coming back to awareness again. As I re-awakened to view the screen of my consciousness behind closed eyes, the candle flame had transformed into a beautiful magenta lotus flower, appearing from the side view, almost like a photograph taken with the blossom at eye level. The magenta was a radiant color, vibrant as though alive, much like the chakra colors (energy centers) when I have been privileged to perceive them—almost electric with energy and like liquid light. The flower and

32

petals were outlined in black, giving the flower a geometric quality, and circling around the outside was a wheel of closely strung, tiny black beads. I discovered I could cause the circle of beads to spin around in either direction and could speed them up or slow them down through mere intent. The lotus remained still and always at center.

Over a period of about a year or so this vision appeared whenever I meditated using a candle (in Sanskrit, the language of India, the term is "Tratak" meaning one-pointed focus). I felt a presence as though the lotus was a live entity and observed me as I observed it. I believe I was connecting with my Higher or Inner Self through this technique and of course with a little study, the symbolism of the lotus became apparent. Because the lotus flower grows its roots in murky pond waters, the stem, winding its way to the surface and the flower blooming gloriously, is untouched by impurity. It represents a metaphor signifying the potential of the enlightened human ascending to embody divinity on earth. I felt like this lotus was a friend, always there when I went to meet it.

Related to this meditation, a couple of clairvoyant channelers I had met in the past told me that they saw a beautiful Goddess accompanying me. They explained that she is like a guardian, supporting me through much of this earthly journey. I was long mildly curious to know which Goddess she was, but never received an answer until many years after my initial lotus meditations. I learned that she is the Goddess Lakshmi, the Indian Goddess of wealth, abundance and good fortune. After investigating the significance of the lotus flower, I found artwork of Lakshmi on the internet. Moving in closer to see her picture on the screen, I exclaimed, "Oh is *that* who you are!" I immediately received a wave of intense, tingling energy throughout my entire body as a sign of confirmation. In my research, I learned that the lotus is sacred to Lakshmi, and she is frequently portrayed sitting on a magenta lotus! To this day, when I close my eyes to meditate, I can see the wheel of beads, I suspect representing the Wheel of Life, and I can still spin it in either direction, faster or slower. This vision may have been an early inner prompt to practice operating from both left and right hemispheres of my brain, perhaps to cultivate whole-brain thinking. Or the spinning beads may represent the spinning chakra wheels. Time will tell, all will unfold as is meant.

# 7 EXPANSION, ACCEPTANCE AND ONENESS

Expanding my studies to other books and practices, I read self-help books, Yoga manuals, metaphysical philosophies, and in 1985 I went for my first reading with the well-known astrologer, Buz Myers. Buz was so well versed in astrology that he spit out astrological terms like water from a fountain. He told me about some of my "past lives" and what some of my strengths and challenges were in this life. Buz said I am a "psychic receptive tool" and that I was the repository for anger in my family dynamics. That rang true. He said my psychic receptivity was like a sponge, and I absorbed everything around me, especially other people's emotions and that I needed to protect myself. He said my family "beat my bloody brains out emotionally—just like a punching bag." That felt right with the spankings, slaps in the face and screaming at me. He also said that my mother was a mirror for me, and as I came to accept and love her, I would love and accept myself. That seemed equal to climbing Mt. Everest or Kilimanjaro.

My reading was so interesting that I transcribed my tape of it and began to study astrology starting with my own chart. It was fascinating. Buz could see in my chart where there had been abuse and even knew at what age. He told me I should develop my natural psychic receptivity and learn to send other people's emotions back to them. He saw my connection with the Cetacean consciousness (whales, dolphins, marine mammals) and thought I would be a natural at channeling. (Channeling, in case you do not already know, is when a person "takes dictation" or lowers down into trance and speaks from a non-physical entity. If the person channeling has cleared their emotional baggage and false belief systems, they can bring through amazingly accurate information and beauty.) As I studied my reading in relation to my experiences, I gained much insight and went for more education on psychic self-defense.

The first metaphysical book I digested was "The Edgar Cayce Primer—Discovering The Path to Self-Transformation," by Herbert B. Puryear, Ph.D. When I worked my first job in downtown Cleveland, there was a coffee shop on the main floor with a book and magazine rack. My hairdresser out in the suburbs told me about this book, and there it appeared in the downtown Cleveland coffee shop. It must have been Divine Intervention because there were no other metaphysical books on the rack. I looked through the book and returned it to its shelf. I went back several times, consternating over whether or not to make the purchase. It was so far from what I had been taught, I felt a nerve-jangling fear as I scanned it, and yet I was drawn to it. Finally, after weeks of wavering, I bought the book. It was more spine-tingling than any psychological thriller I had ever read or watched.

Dr. Puryear discusses truths based on Edgar Cayce's life as the well-known "sleeping prophet." He discusses psychicism, spirituality and God, dreams, the occult, the nature of reality, emotions, and reincarnation. I literally shook when I read about the illusions of duality—and yet I knew it resonated as truth for me. I was terrified that God would strike me down if I opened to these ideas, the same God I feared if I slept without a sheet at night causing me to feel vulnerable to attack. Having unconsciously started my search for Truth while still in high school, during lucid moments, I knew something was wrong. I once convinced my father to take me to the preacher of our church to inquire about what Truth might be. That discussion turned into a mere social visit with no further insight than that which I began. Having seen a counselor around the time of the suicide attempt, an anger management facilitator, and an astrologer, now, while reading this book, the pieces were starting to fit together. I realized I had much work to do on myself to expand my awareness further and open more to my current life, memories from other lifestreams (commonly known as "past lives"), and spirituality without the restrictions and prefabricated structures of parents and manmade religion. I continued on my search, devouring books on psychology and spiritual topics from several cultures. I remained in deep relationship with my beloved Yoga and meditation.

During the first several years I practiced Yoga and meditation, I was fortunate to have some beautiful experiences. However, at first, I did find that having such an active mind was quite a challenge. It could take me up to two hours to calm my mind sufficiently to even approach a meaningful experience. Yoga helped me to relax my body, but my mind wandered through a seemingly endless supply of distractions pulling me from my center.

These early meditations, beginning with the usual relaxation period, soon filled my mind with visual images resembling those experienced in dreams. As I watched, parades of medieval people marched and milled about on the screen of my inner vision. I saw many Christian crosses, decorated with filigree and fancy edges, being carried and waved around like flags. I saw so many in such frequency that I finally asked in meditation, "What do these crosses mean?" My curiosity was intense to the extent that I lay down on my bed in *Savasana* (the Yoga relaxation pose) informing my Higher Self that I would remain there until I received an answer. The answer that came almost immediately was, "this is the 'Mystic cross'." The energy that seared through my body as I received this answer was powerful, almost shocking. I then wondered what a "mystic" was and began to investigate. I presumed that at the spiritual level I planned to walk the mystic path and decided to allow my journey to unfold.

After a month or so, I did not see the crosses any more—perhaps because I "got" the message. In their place, I saw a white, tuba-shaped form lying with its opening facing upward that drew me toward it. I intuitively knew I should dive into the circular aperture with my consciousness. Whenever I did make that dive, I would go deeper into meditation and some sort of imagery would emerge. I believe these forms appeared for the purpose of drawing me deeper into an altered state, so I could receive information and integrate my life-lessons and divinity.

As I continued meditating, I learned it is even possible to receive Love from a presence in the unseen world. Indeed, we can receive Love from our Guardians on a daily basis. In one such meditation, I received two gifts: a Divine presence emanating acceptance, comfort and compassion and an answer to a puzzling question regarding how to proceed with my career. This is how it went.

One afternoon, while practicing Yoga alone in my living room, graced by the company of my cat, I felt certain that I was a source of entertainment for my female feline friend who observed me with a seemingly amused expression on her furry black face. I fantasized that she might think I should reincarnate as Cat in order to execute some of the poses. I wondered in humor if I could somehow be injected with an elixir of feline flexibility as I directed my body through some of the more challenging *asanas*. Later on, it was my body directing me through the *asanas* as I explored the intelligence of this physical form and its relationship with

*Prana* (vital life force, *aka* Chi). On this Saturday, I practiced my *asanas* in a quiet setting, with late afternoon sun streaming in through the windows, all uneventful until I stretched out on my back for *Savasana*. I relaxed, melting into the floor for a few minutes, simply staring at the blank screen of the inside of my eyelids, when I noticed an image beginning to unfold. It looked as though a scroll was being deliberately, slowly unrolled from the top down. At the top, I saw the crown of someone's head with hair tousled a bit, then a forehead, and eyebrows. Next, I saw large, dark eyes, and as the scroll unrolled further, there was the remainder of a face covered by a beard. It was Jesus. His eyes were like those of a fawn--soft, deep pools, gazing at me with a sort of detached compassion, an assumed acceptance of me. I just lay there looking at this image posted on the entire screen of my mind, part of me wondering why he had come and how I should respond. I simply waited without communicating anything except for mentally raising my eyebrows, posing my query. Then I heard him in my mind relay to me, "Just keep doing what you're doing." Since I had been in quite a quandary about whether or not to continue teaching Yoga full-time, I could interpret his comment as an answer in the affirmative. Or perhaps he was intimating that I was to keep working on my self-healing. Often, in an either/or scenario, both answers are correct. I did both. I did not experience any earth-shattering elevation of my consciousness or shocking mind expansion into the Universe. I did not feel overcome by dramatic emotion or realize any major life secret. Often we do not enter meditation with a goal or expectation; that attachment can close down opportunity much like a grabbing hand. But if one asks for an answer and then detaches and *allows* the answer, it often comes, or it may surface later like in a title to an article of a magazine that we intuitively know fits.

This meditation has been a source of comfort to me ever since I experienced the unfolding of the image. I know Jesus exists within me, and I can call on Him at any time, including during times of trial. The feeling of His acceptance, with all my idiosyncrasies and faults in plain view (I could sense He knew me), has assisted me with my own self-acceptance. Finding acceptance from a Guide or Higher Self is one of the advantages to meditation and anyone can have spiritual experiences or find peace within. It is possible to unearth answers in meditation because that is where they emanate--from within. After all, we are spiritual beings having a human experience.

Another significant early meditation occurred with clear dream-like visual images; I pondered its meaning for twenty years. To keep track of these messages, I kept a meditation/dream journal, which helped me look for patterns of imbalance or unrecognized talents, like putting together pieces of a puzzle. It turns out that this meditation actually revealed part of my life's purpose. No one outside of myself could possibly give me that.

The meditation happened in 1985, the year I began teaching Yoga and deepened my meditation practice. I had a vision where I found myself out west somewhere, alone in the desert. The sun was shining, and the earth appeared dry and barren. As I looked around, I saw a huge chasm in the earth as though it had partially split in two; I walked over to explore it. It appeared to be a split deep into the earth, like two cliffs had separated exposing the earth's center. Straddling the chasm with one foot placed on each side, I looked down inside it and simply said, "Helloooooo." Instantly, the chasm slammed shut leaving no trace of even a crack. Soon, my spiritual Guardians channeled telling me they did not know how else to relay this information, saying that it did not mean earth healing.

It took twenty years of periodic pondering to receive the understanding of this meditation. Through contemplation, I now understand it has to do with my "voice," the tone of my soul. The tone of my soul, my expression, is to bridge the opposites--the two sides of the chasm. Through the voice of my teaching, my way of being as I achieve greater centering and balance, I am helping others to come into their center or balance. Key factors are both my physical voice and my voice of expression. People have often commented on my speaking voice during Yoga, saying it is soothing and relaxing. When in mere conversation with a person who is not acclimated to being relaxed, they will literally fall asleep at the sound of my voice. I have found over the years since I started teaching Yoga that people who are over-stimulated and rushing much of the time or do not get enough deep sleep lose their experience of relaxation. They do not even relax during sleep. They are the ones that fall asleep when I speak. There is sometimes an effect on the voice from many years of practicing Yoga—it is actually called "the Yoga voice." Perhaps that is what the meditation referred to, the vibration of the Yogi or Yogini's voice, a female Yoga practitioner. I do know that I transmit the energy of Yoga and transformation, and it is possible that it comes through on the sound vibration of my voice. I also have directed my voice in chanting OM toward the Earth's tectonic plates to help relieve stress in those areas.

In addition, I believe that the meditation refers to the separation that occurs when we split off from parts of ourselves causing an emotional and spiritual chasm from others, Nature, and All That Is. Yoga reconnects us. The word "Yoga" comes from the Sanskrit "Yug", to hitch up. We are all One, and we need to return to that Connection. I find Yoga, including meditation, is the perfect discipline to accomplish this task of re-Connection. The Yoga *asanas* with breathing techniques (Pranayama) bring light to our bodies all the way down to the cellular level. Meditation allows the fluctuations of the mind to come to rest rather than swinging back and forth between the opposites. Meditation connects the two sides of the chasm; the good/bad, arrogance/low self-esteem, reverence/irreverence, Light/Dark, restlessness/stillness, excitement/boredom, active/passive, love/fear, and so on. We reconnect with Divine Love, express Divine Love from our heart space and maybe even ignite the spark in others. I have come to recognize that God is everything, even me. Now, that is a far cry from suicide, would you not agree?

# 8 INNER EXPLORATION – MEETING UNSEEN FRIENDS

After I began teaching Yoga on a full-time basis in 1985, I spent a lot of time in meditation, for three reasons: 1) I wanted to achieve Peace, 2) I had the time available since I was not working in an office any more, and 3) I felt pulled inside from some need to explore my inner landscape. Those were my reasons, in addition to the fact that meditation is a part of Yoga. I was inspired by Paramahansa Yogananda's book, <u>Autobiography of a Yogi</u>, a classic writing revealing the amazing experiences of his life. While I still had a lot of difficulty communicating with people and intimacy was as elusive as a butterfly, I felt comforted through the meditative process and I did find answers to questions, some questions I had not even posed yet.

A profound vision of an aspect of myself was revealed to me on a spring day when my friend Paul and I had been racing along the bike path in the Metro parks. It was particularly fun when Paul would ride up beside me, slap his hand onto my shoulder and nonchalantly hang on while I pedaled for both of us. It simply struck my "funny bone" for some reason. Paul and I met on the bike path during a rest break sitting on a bench overlooking a pond next to the trail. We considered it a prime spot for a rest and shared it many times. It was a ten-mile ride to the bench making it a good place to turn around and head for home. This was one of those times filled with laughter and lightheartedness. We rode back to my apartment a short distance from the entrance to the park. We both were pleasantly tired and decided to lie down for a nap. Just after I lay down, I felt prompted by intuition to get up and meditate with the candle. I had been working with meditation exercises in <u>The Miracle of Metaphysical Healing</u> by Evelyn M. Monahan (July 1977), a book that instructed the reader to unequivocally command the Higher Self to make an appearance or to otherwise make itself known. I had been stating that command for a few weeks. During this candle meditation, the flame morphed into a spinning circle with the beads around it as usual, and the center kept swirling like a whirlpool of pure energy. Then suddenly the circle abruptly shrunk when a huge, vibrantly red triangle blasted like a rocket onto the screen of my mind's eye. The now tiny candle flame/circle quickly floated up inside the apex, like the eye of the pyramid on the one-dollar bill only this one not a human eye—more like an energy eye. The pyramid was bursting with vibrant red energy like a living, pulsing explosion. I could feel its presence and power. I could actually see its power as it radiated before me, feeling like I was peering into a vast expanse. My first reaction to its presence was surprise perceiving it as a live being without any arms. It startled me to the point that I momentarily opened my eyes. I did not want to miss anything, so I closed my eyes again and the triangle reappeared as before, the "eye"-flame still whirling and glowing, a smaller version of what I would usually see when practicing candle meditation. I intuitively understood that this was a form representing my Higher Self in response to my commands, and that I am its physical arms. I had the distinct impression that I am to allow its expression through me, my arms and hands.

Eventually the form evaporated and I was left with a sense of awe and wonder. Part of me knew what it was and another part of me sat wondering what the heck just happened. I felt compelled to work with pyramid power after that and was very careful about what I commanded from my Higher Self. Even now I visualize various sizes of pyramids for protection over my living space, car and body. I also still visualize the red triangle from time to time, but it has never appeared as the living red "being" that exploded onto the screen of my mind's eye that day. Many years later as I continued the study of my astrology chart, I discovered there is within it a "grand fire trine," representing ease and flow to express creatively and to live through enthusiasm and joy. I believe this grand fire trine relates to my meditation where I viewed the vibrant red triangle in my mind's eye. This is how I am to express my very soul—creatively and with joy and enthusiasm—and my chart's energy supports me. At the time, that seemed like a tall order. Perhaps I would grow into my trine, or make good use of its energy whenever it was lit up or triggered.

On the path of growth then, one weekend evening later that spring, it seemed all my friends were unavailable and I was feeling lonely and abandoned so I collapsed into a vat of self-pity. It would seem nobler that I would practice Yoga out of the sheer love for it, but that night I took to my mat out of pure need for release. At first, my efforts felt like I was moving through mud. I had to stoke my inner fire (solar plexus) to burn away sluggishness and dross. After a couple of hours, through the transformational power of the asanas, the feeling of peace washed over me as I lay in Corpse Pose (Savasana - relaxation). When prompted from within to come out of the pose, it was around ten o'clock, time for bed. I decided to assume Corpse Pose lying in bed until I fell asleep, hoping to deepen my relaxation as I crept unconsciously into the night. The last thing I remember thinking before falling asleep was, "I need comforting."

Later in the night, I awoke as I lay on my back more relaxed than I had ever been before, with arms at my sides and palms turned upward, still in Savasana. I had not moved. I peered down towards my feet. I was hovering just above my body and was seeing it from a slightly higher perspective than normal. It was the middle of the night yet the entire room glowed mysteriously with a thick, golden, cloud-like energy or light (the same golden energy I saw when I was in the anger management support group). I felt someone holding my right hand, and the sensation of comfort streaming into me.

I looked over to my right and there I saw a woman. She appeared to be a grandmotherly type with smooth, plump features and her white hair was drawn up into a bun. Her eyes were closed and she hinted at a smile like the one you might see on the face of a Buddha or Quan Yin statue. She was an apparition in opaque white, but I could see her dark colored dress was printed with light flowers on it. She appeared to be seated and was positioned next to the right side of my bed near the foot, but I did not see any chair or other support underneath her. Nor could I see her hand touching mine, but that is what I felt, yet her hands appeared to be folded in her lap. I tried to speak to her, but my mouth refused to move. It simply would not open. I felt as though I was being forced to speak with her telepathically. I exclaimed my "thought" to her, "You're comforting me! " There was no response from her, no movement of her form. But what happened next seemed to me superior to words and I believe a communication from her that conveyed volumes.

I felt a gentle tingling in my toes which began to travel slowly up my feet and into my legs, increasing in intensity as it moved. Once the energy reached my knees, it accelerated, racing up the rest of my body to the top of my head with a whoosh. It felt wonderfully stimulating and energizing, but also peaceful. I sent my thought to her how stimulating it was, knowing she was the director of this energy. Then I felt the tingling again. I began to feel shy, wondering about the appearance of an apparition appearing in the middle of the night. I noticed myself entering "avoidance" mode and as I turned to lie on my side facing away from her, I relayed the half-truth to her

42

that I was tired and going back to sleep. Somehow I knew she understood. I have not seen her since, consciously at least, nor in that form. But it seems the tingling and comforting energy she brought me are always available at a moment's notice.

The next day when I played racquetball with my friend Holly, I could do no wrong. I intuitively knew where to stand to serve, where to aim my serve and how to return her volleys. It was great. I felt as though not only was I playing racquetball with my friend, but I also was playing with my spirit guides or Higher Self. I could feel Guidance' direction the entire time. This must be what it is like to be "in the zone" as athletes claim. Later in the day, relaxation and play gave way to anxiety as I thought about my ethereal experience with my ghostly evening visitor. I reasoned if there are invisible forces that can bring comfort, there must be invisible forces or beings that are capable of harming me. My Baptist upbringing kicked in and I lost my mellow mood in exchange for fear and hyper vigilance. I was finding this expansion of self, mind, whatever it was called, downright scary. Nightmares returned to haunt me into feeling powerless. One dream I had showed me standing in a line of prisoners before a firing squad and I was killed. It was time to employ more psychic self-defense techniques and I worked with the White Light for protection, though I was not certain I believed in its effectiveness. I had more to learn.

I continued meditating regularly and met my Spirit Guide, Karl, who meditated with me. I could perceive him sitting across from me during meditation. At the end of my meditations with him, I could feel my chakras (energy centers) spinning very fast. It felt as though the energy from my chakras was merging into one point in front of me, and moving forward, toward Karl. The love and peace I felt was very satisfying and heartwarming. It felt like the intensity of the love we were sharing caused my chakras to spin much faster.

Frequently in meditations I met a beautiful woman who always wore a hat. She conveyed to me that she lives on the planet Venus, her name is Elizabeth and told me we would one day write books together. I even saw a huge eye of a whale in another meditation. Other times I would see many people passing across my screen of vision. When I asked Spirit who these people were, I received the response that they were my friends on the other side of the veil. I was still experiencing quite a bit of isolation at this time, and was very introspective and focused on Yoga and meditation. These friends were helping me to feel connected, providing relating on the inner planes during this period of enforced solitude.

In one very significant meditation, I met a man who appeared in my vision dressed in a businessman's suit with hair very conservatively cut and styled. He wore very large, dark-rimmed glasses and evoked within me a feeling of incredible love, though I did not consciously know who he was. He was playfully flirtatious and somehow I recognized him, but did not know from where. I felt a very strong attraction to him. The man motioned through hand gestures and a charming, mischievous expression for me to come along with him. He approached a set of stairs that were ascending from just right of center (viewed from the side of the stairs). As he climbed the steps, I could not see where he was going as nothing was shown, he was headed into the unknown perhaps. Even though I very much wanted to follow him up the stairs, I felt hesitant. I never saw him again in my meditations—in that form. But I thought about him--wondering who he was, where the steps were leading, why I felt afraid to accompany him--and why I felt so attracted to him. I put the issue on the proverbial stack of "all things to be revealed in good time" and moved on.

After this meditation, I somehow sensed more love around me and began to wonder if I was going to meet a man soon. I learned several years later that the stairs were a metaphor for rising into "higher consciousness" and seeming to lead to nowhere, they were actually leading into the "unknown." I felt anxious because my egoic or conditioned self would have to be surrendered, revealing my authentic self, and trust was an intense issue for me (remember that decision at five years?). Walking the path to higher consciousness meant leaving the comfort of the *status quo*, and embarking on a journey into the unknown. I believe this is the journey that strikes fear into the heart of everyone. I was soon to learn exactly what that meant.

As I continued teaching Yoga, I periodically searched for additional opportunities for places to offer my classes. One of my students relayed to me her discovery of a new metaphysical center opening just a few miles west of where I lived. I asked the Universe to confirm the information knowing that if it was appropriate for me to teach there, I would receive a sign. It came unusually quickly--the next day. I was racing along the bike path through the Metro Park when I decided to exit up the hill leading into the town where a good friend practiced law. I stopped in to chat and after a short visit, decided to head back home—a ten-mile ride. My friend escorted me out as I left his office. While we walked, he mentioned reading an article in the newspaper announcing a new metaphysical center opening fairly close to my home. He nonchalantly asked if I was going to teach there. I recognized this as my sign and wasted no time pedaling home to explore the opportunity.

# I Forgive You, Daddy – Yoga and the Angels Healed Me!

I felt a sense of urgency to get myself ready to stop by the new center. On my way driving to the place, I headed towards a red glowing sun that seemed to hang in the western sky, making it a beautiful and pleasant drive. "The White Light" metaphysical center was a two-story house that had been converted into an office with a few small classrooms. A gift shop just inside the front entrance displayed a colorful array of gems and crystals and an assortment of jewelry. The door was open so I went in and looked around for someone to ask about offering Yoga classes. There was only one person to be found--a young woman who said she would be teaching psychic development. She displayed a delightful personality—upbeat, enthusiastic and somewhat innocent and childlike. She said she also worked as a trance channeler allowing several different entities to speak through her while she was in a state of deep meditation or trance, the main attraction being an angel named Merishkan. His name was Abcei-Merishkan, but most called him Merishkan. Hearing all this made me feel a little uncomfortable, as I was only vaguely familiar with the channeling process. I could trust in angels, but channeling, metaphorically letting someone else take the keys and drive, was a little foreign to me. I found the psychic world intriguing; however, it did provoke a slight uneasiness. I suppose that is the nature of the unknown.

The young woman's name was Susan Marie, but she called herself Coyote. She explained that her guides gave her that name in meditation. (The name "Coyote" was a clue to suggest the role she would eventually play in my life—I was mildly cautious.) Nonetheless, I was fascinated and pushed any discomfort aside at least temporarily to allow the scenario to unfold. Coyote told me she could see auras and that mine was yellow, similar to other committed Yoga practitioners she had met. She said that in her experience it seemed all Yoga practitioners had yellow auras. I resisted the temptation for the time being to ask what that meant. As we talked, she showed me around the downstairs of the Center with the tour ending in the kitchen. At this point, the woman who opened the new center arrived and Coyote announced to her that their new Yoga teacher had arrived. I felt the woman trusted Coyote's judgment and ability to read people, though she herself seemed to want credit for the assessment of me. I did not feel the same trustworthiness and innocence in her but felt that there was no harm in teaching Yoga classes in her new facility.

Within a short while I began teaching Yoga at the White Light Center. Even the main classrooms were small, but that allowed for more intimate classes--teaching was great fun for me. Coyote and I became closer friends through hours of conversation over after-class coffee. We shared a love of the metaphysical and philosophical realms. She mentioned someone named

Merishkan frequently and referred to telepathically communicating with him even as she talked with me. Her psychic gifts were readily apparent. She would pull information seemingly out of thin air as she easily tapped into the Akashic records, the "library in the sky." Since I was unfamiliar with the channeling process, I felt a twinge of nervousness, but trusted there was nothing really to fear. Coyote had not channeled in my presence yet, but I knew that was just a matter of time—she loved to channel. I remember how the feeling of bliss lingered after teaching Yoga and how delightful it was to have someone with whom to chat about spiritual matters after Yoga. I was learning to trust her as a friend.

The woman who owned the White Light Center and Coyote received an invitation to be featured at a psychic party in a nearby suburb. I planned to attend the party and became highly enthused about it. A friend who was a highly successful financial planner was hosting this party, lending some credibility to the event. My intuition was strongly advising me it was important for me to attend, that I was going to meet the man of my life, and that two of my closer friends would also find it important to attend. There was something happening—somehow I knew this party would change my life. My one friend Julie was planning to be out of town that weekend but changed her plans through my persuasion. Another friend of mine was excited about the party as she was fascinated by psychicism; she was naturally psychic herself. The owner of the Center claimed to be psychic and would conduct readings and Coyote was planning to channel Merishkan sometime during the evening of the party. All I had to do was to wait a month until the date of the party. Patience never was my strong suit and anticipation continued to build as Coyote and I maintained our discussions, cementing a new friendship. Somehow I could feel myself awakening and becoming more energetic as time for the party slowly approached. Having recently received an income tax refund, I decided to buy a new outfit for the event. I felt incredibly inspired.

The day of the party finally arrived. It was being held at a community center in a luxury apartment complex where my financial planner friend lived. He had made all the arrangements. I felt such energy coursing through me in a calm yet stimulating flow to the extent that my face was flushed like a new bride. I drove alone to the complex and found my way to the party center. There were already about forty people there and I scanned the room for my friends. I saw Coyote sitting in a chair across the center of the room. I did not see my other friends yet so I milled around for a while feeling a sense of anticipation and high energy. The atmosphere in the room was electric. It would take time for me to understand what was really happening.

# I Forgive You, Daddy – Yoga and the Angels Healed Me!

Eventually everyone settled down finding seats in a circle around Coyote, so I knew she was about to channel. I had seen channeling twice before when it caused strange sensations within me, so I was slightly apprehensive. Coyote sat still in an upholstered armchair and effortlessly dropped into a trance with her eyes closed. Soon she opened her eyes and someone else was speaking through her. The expression in her eyes changed, her mannerisms changed and her voice was deep and fairly guttural. People were going up to Coyote to ask questions so I moved in closer to hear more clearly. Merishkan was channeling through. Finally I was getting to meet the revered Merishkan. I felt a strong sense of love and energy emanating from him and was attracted to it like a moth to light. He announced he would clear auric fields and balance chakras for anyone who was interested. I was interested. I also felt nervous--timid but highly curious. A fellow moved to sit in front of Merishkan for his balancing and cleansing. He told the fellow he was already in balance and that it was due to his discipline of practicing Yoga. That did it. I practiced a lot of Yoga and wanted to see what Merishkan had to say about me. Walking towards him, I watched as someone else went to sit in front of him for a balancing. I moved into position so I could be next in line.

When it came my turn, I sat kneeling on the floor in front of Merishkan; my face must have been crimson by now. I introduced myself and with a knowing twinkle in his eyes he stated he knew who I was. All kinds of feelings were searing through my body: excitement—anxiety—anticipation—adoration. He asked, "What can I do for you?" Now I *know* my face was crimson; I felt self-conscious and embarrassed. He had just stated that we could come up and receive aura and chakra balancing. Why this question? "I just wanted you to check out my aura," I responded. Even though I usually speak in softer tones, my voice always sounds loud to me from inside my head. Now as I blurted out my request, I was emphatic sufficiently to cause Merishkan to blink. I felt more embarrassed. He was nonetheless unaffected by my assertion and proceeded to check my aura. He stated that I was already in balance and again affirmed that my aura was yellow, whatever that meant. I wondered how, with my being nervous, full of self-doubts, low self-esteem and fear I could possibly appear to be in balance. And yet, with the love pouring forth from him, and me as well, I was electrified by romance at that moment. Perhaps the immense love I was feeling eclipsed any self-doubts or low self-esteem.

Feeling radiant with the crimson in my face beaming like neon, I left Merishkan and the party to go outdoors for some fresh air. I needed to integrate what had just happened. I talked with a couple of others who were also taking in the beauty of the grounds. Once I returned, the rest of the party was uneventful. Merishkan remained in channel for quite a while and I wondered where Coyote went when he was speaking through her. The Center's owner performed a reading and told another friend and me that we were twins in another life—that was interesting as we have the same birthday in this life. The owner did a few other short readings, but appeared to be indulging in drugs and alcohol. She had arrived late in a limousine with several young men and left the party early. I had the feeling the Center might be in trouble. And my attraction to Merishkan was not going away.

After arriving home, I turned in still thinking about Merishkan and the feelings he elicited in me. I restlessly tossed and turned all night. I kept hearing Merishkan's name echoing in my head--all the next night too. I wondered about so many things. For instance, being out of channel, did he come around me from Spirit side? I both hoped so and was afraid it might be.

Coyote confirmed my intuition about trouble brewing at the Center. She was actually sharing living space with the woman who ran the Center and her much younger boyfriend. She told me a few days later about their indulgence in drugs and how disturbing it was to be a psychic sensitive living there. Coyote also believed that drugs were being sold in the parking lot behind the Center. I lived in a one-bedroom apartment and began thinking that my couch might be suitable for Coyote to sleep on if she needed a temporary place to stay. I conceivably could accommodate her for a while. I decided to take more time to think about it rather than make an impulsive decision. In the meantime, we were both considering severing ties with the White Light Center. I was receiving income from other teaching positions and could manage without the small classes held there. We still were cementing our friendship through many hours of discussions about metaphysics, philosophy, reality and truth. Time didn't exist during these exchanges. Coyote did not channel Merishkan around me; perhaps she could sense my slight uneasiness.

Within a couple of weeks, after hearing more about the challenges with her living situation, I decided it might be a good idea to offer help to Coyote. I offered her a place to stay; she was delighted and relieved. She said she did not have a lot of possessions so would not require much space in my place. I only had few possessions too, but then I had always preferred open space.

Once Coyote completed her move into my apartment, she began channeling almost immediately. Not only did she channel Merishkan, but also the Oracle of the Tarot and my own spirit guide, Karl, with whom I had been meditating for some time. That is how I knew the channeling was of high integrity. I recognized Karl in channel, he was the most beautiful entity of all and I loved him dearly. There were many others that spoke through Coyote, human and non-human. Merishkan was always around and began coming through frequently. I had already read the Seth material channeled by Jane Roberts, much of the Edgar Cayce material and many other books about reality and spirituality. Now I felt I was living it.

The love I felt for Merishkan after that first encounter was intense and distracting. He became gently flirtatious in channel and I cherished the times when he came through. I felt like a teenager with a crush. One time when Coyote channeled Merishkan, she was gone for several hours. She loved channeling so she could explore space and the other dimensions; she was a gifted psychic.

During the time when Coyote was gone for several hours, Merishkan and I were left alone together. We went for a peaceful walk along the topside edge of the Metro parks during the warm, summer evening and talked. Our philosophies differed as I expressed my belief that "love is the answer." Merishkan exclaimed, "I *protect* people that believe that way! " I think we had different ideas of what love is and how to express that quality. It was a philosophical difference and I believed time would reveal the truth of the matter. He later asked me, "How would you feel if I were around all the time?" I enthusiastically told him, "I would love it! " We harassed each other some more in good humor eventually returning to the apartment. I was in awe that Coyote could channel for such a long duration.

It was well past midnight when we arrived home. I asked Merishkan what he was thinking at this point about being around all the time since he had asked me my feelings on the matter. He said, "It is done." I was shocked by his response. I asked him with surprise, "What do you mean?" He said he and Coyote were in telepathic rapport as we walked and they discussed trading places. He was here to stay—he was now a "walk-in." Coyote, the original occupant of her physical form removed her soul from the body and Merishkan took up residence. I was both overjoyed and saddened. I had learned to love Coyote as a dear friend and felt I would miss her. The next night after this amazing switch, Merishkan channeled Coyote. The situation was becoming complex and my head was spinning, but I adored Merishkan and felt a deep trust of the situation, even though dotted with some discomfort due to my unfamiliarity with such phenomena. Information gradually unfolded that we had been mates in many life streams. No wonder I felt so much love for him--our bond spanned beyond the confines of linear time and space.

How would I ever have guessed the man of my life would turn out to be

49

non-human? He appeared in my meditation as a businessman so I would be comfortable, but he was definitely not human. Channeling would reveal that Merishkan is a silver angel sent by higher beings to help with Humanity's growth. How exciting--Merishkan now would be around all the time and my friend Coyote channeled through him so there was no sense of loss.

Now, about those stairs leading into the unknown...

# 9 LET HEALING BEGIN!

Shortly after Merishkan "walked-in," my guide Karl spoke through him informing me that Merishkan had been sent under the auspices of the goddess Kali to connect energy lines to me and a couple other people for future use. This all happened in the summer of 1986, the year before the Harmonic Convergence in August of 1987. I was 39 years old, just a few months before turning 40, the significance of which will become readily apparent. My understanding of the Harmonic Convergence is that the Human Collective decided to turn away from negativity, to not let the planet be annihilated as was the original plan to end our Human "game" and to create a new reality. One tall order!   The code for this event is recorded in the DNA of every human as 11:11. When you see that number, pay attention and visualize what you want in your life. It is important.

Merishkan and I became good friends with Julie, a young woman I met when I lead Yoga classes at the local YMCA. She and I connected not only on the Yogic level, but we felt we had known each other before. We chatted about Yoga, the Runes, astrology and other types of studies. All three of us felt close to each other and we got together often, for channeling, Tarot readings and playing with our psychic abilities. After a couple of months with Merishkan staying at my apartment, a house came open for rent and we went to see it. My friend who had the same birthday that attended the psychic party found it and had moved into the in-law's suite upstairs. Merishkan, Julie and I looked at the downstairs. There was plenty of room and we fell in love with the house and yard. We all three moved in and Merishkan channeled Susie, the house spirit. Homes, cars, buildings—all have a spirit to maintain the energy of the structure. Susie knew I was good at housecleaning and would "nudge" me when it came time to clean. I would feel a strong urge and she would "shine" when I heard her and took action at her prompting. She told us that I represented the house, Merishkan the yard and Julie the windows. Julie felt slighted that she represented mere windows, but Susie said, "If you believe anyone can live without windows, better think again! " I agreed, having worked in office buildings where only the authorities or bosses were privileged to have windows. One large firm did, however, have a lunchroom on the forty-something floor that had floor-to-ceiling windows overlooking Lake Erie. It was a breathtaking view, so I ate lunch and took breaks there as often as I could. Yes, windows are extremely important. The three of us formed a triangle, important to the flow of energy which was useful during the channeling and for the upcoming work we would be carrying out.

Merishkan had channeled the Over-soul of the Cetacean Consciousness (the "Higher Self" of the group soul of all marine mammals in the world) and this entity told me I would channel them due to our spiritual connection. Buz Myers the astrologer I mentioned earlier told me that I had been a sailor in more lifetimes than I could count. He said that I was a hunter probably in the Inuit tribe in the icy north and hunted whales—but honorably. That meant that I was an honorable person with high integrity and the whales sought me out to share their bodies with me and my family (similar to the Native American Indians). When I would hunt and kill the whale, its spirit would then come into my being and I would honor the animal as revered and worthy of respect. Also, when I was a sailor I would stand near the railing on deck and when the dolphins came, I would astral project (send my consciousness) into the water and play with the dolphins. The channeled whale entity said I would channel them when I was ready. I did some of that work, meditating with the over-soul entity and then writing about it on the computer, but with the business of healing my life and earning a living, the project has been on the back burner. (Perhaps that will be my *next* writing project!)

Excavation of my soul began immediately. My guide Karl channeled through Merishkan and told me it would be necessary for me to go back to work in the office. He said that with the depth of transformation I was about to experience, it would not be wise to take students through it. Just being in class with me would have an impact and pulling back on my Yoga classes was out of consideration for their highest good and wellbeing. The students that were capable of handling this energy could still attend my classes—it was a natural transition. The ones that were better off abstaining from my classes temporarily simply did not show up. Once I completed my journey, I would be better equipped to assist them on their journeys. Little did I know this transformation, this deep soul cleansing, even for the *initial stages*, would last 15 years! I learned this in casual conversation with

Merishkan about the duration of the changes I was facing. In truth, with my astrology chart showing 3 planets and 2 asteroids in the sign of investigative, probing and passionate Scorpio, all crammed into the 5th house of creativity, love given, creative outlets, and more, transformation would never really be over! The intensity might lighten up and I would eventually learn to embrace transformation with more ease; even finding it fun. However, at the daunting precipice of this journey, I felt like I was going kicking and screaming. But I was going, nonetheless. At a higher level, I had agreed to it.

It was a very interesting phenomenon, a *non-human, Higher Self spirit guide* speaking through a "walk-in" *angelic being* housed in a *human's* physical form—we used to joke about the revolving door of that body's consciousness. Later, it would not seem so humorous.

At any rate, facing a return to office life was disappointing news since it was stressful for me to work in downtown Cleveland which at that time was a very "dark" energy and for unsympathetic, often hostile attorneys who were demanding with the workload and quite generous with their critical putdowns. Just putting on pantyhose and getting to work in the city seemed like a job in itself. With a minus 10 on the confidence scale, and feeling the constant urge to be free, I had an extremely difficult time tolerating this type of environment. But the guides told me I was taking Spirit, a band of Angels, into the offices where I worked assisting with the cause of enlightenment, they said, more than I knew.

It was always a delight when I came home since Merishkan had great cooking skills and created tasty, nutritious meals. He infused love into our meals which supported the healing work we were doing. We had a great time playing with the Tarot, which initially made me anxious, but I eventually learned from the Tarot Oracle since Merishkan often channeled her as we did readings and study every evening. I soon learned that since I was working with unseen forces (angels, spirit guides, even extra-terrestrials, Gaia/Earth Mother) they accompanied me into the offices where I worked and brought the Light of the Divine into the city. I learned to call on them and ask for support which was always met with reinforcement. In my travels, I had met a couple other Yoga teachers working in downtown offices too, so I suspect on the Spiritual plane, we were all working together. In addition, while I was building the emotional strength to stand up for myself, I became an agent of change and reported injustices that brought awareness and elevated vibrations wherever I worked. Acting as an agent for change was terrifying for me as I detested confrontation and most of the time felt like hiding rather than taking action. Claiming my power back was only one of my lessons this lifetime. All would unfold.

Soon I accepted a legal office professional position working for a 70-year-old managing partner at a small firm in the Terminal Tower in downtown. He was ill and did not feel well most of the time. Just after starting the job, I had a premonition that he would die within 6 months. He used to stand in front of me, in an open office occupied by clerical co-workers as well as attorneys, and angrily screamed at me about what a poor job I was doing and how I worked at a snail's pace. I felt such embarrassment and humiliation. The firm had a new, state-of-the-art computer for all workers and I was working as fast as I could to learn it. This attorney would dictate the minutes of the board meetings to me as I recorded in shorthand, but reading some of the material from the previous meeting or from some other typed text at what seemed like break-neck speed. I repeatedly asked him to slow down, and he did for a couple of sentences, soon returning to his former speed. I was trained in shorthand and reached the required speed to graduate with honors from school, but reading the dictation just wasn't fair. Out of desperation, I went to the nearest Radio Shack and bought a voice activated mini-tape recorder. When summoned for dictation, I took it with me, hid it under my steno pad and covered it with a Kleenex tissue--he never caught on. I took dictation to the best of my ability and when I could not hear him or he read too fast, I had the tape recorder as backup. He died after I had worked there 9 months, leaving me to look for another job. My premonition was correct—I even had a couple of dreams with him.

At one job where I was working as a temporary legal assistant, hoping to land a permanent position, it was the secretarial coordinator that was manipulative and abused her authority. I had communicated to her that I was interested in a permanent position. The temp agency sent me to this office, a law firm of about 80 attorneys but I had yet to interview for a permanent position. One day, the supervisor called me on the interoffice phone and advised me that she wanted me to work the day after Thanksgiving when most people would be off. I had already told her in advance that I was unavailable that day and that I had an opportunity to be on cable television to give a demonstration class and talk about Yoga. She told me that she was in the process of setting up interviews with two attorneys needing an assistant and that I had to make a choice between the job and the TV appearance. I was furious as I knew she had not made any such arrangements for me to interview. I chose the TV gig. I wrote a letter to her manager with a copy to the owners of the temporary agency describing her game. In a couple of weeks, I learned that she had gotten into an argument with another temporary legal assistant when in anger she grabbed and tore the girl's blouse. She was fired as soon as that temporary reported her.

The attorneys and coordinators were not the only ones with whom I found challenge. In one law office, I remember receiving orientation that included a meeting with a secretary that had worked for over 20 years at this firm. She was given the responsibility of reviewing with new assistants some of the generally accepted policies and procedures. This woman was very nervous, a bit haughty and treated everyone rather harshly, bordering on meanness. When I sat alone with her in a small conference room, she barked at me some of the rules and then said, "You know the drill," since I also had several years of experience in this field. She then proceeded to touch on a few more policy issues. As I listened intently, I noticed a stream resembling a liquid light laser shooting over my right shoulder toward her. This was not anything I caused... directly. Then she exclaimed to me, "What did you do to me! ?" Something is in my eye! " I calmly smiled and said I did not do anything. Then she abruptly stood up still working to remove something from her right eye, and stalked off to the ladies' room. When she returned, she disclosed that she was wearing contacts. She seemed softer, more humbled at this point and if I remember correctly, she said something about never messing with me. She concluded this part of my orientation and never did "mess with me." I learned later that she had been living with her boyfriend for about 20 years and he abruptly left her. She had two nervous breakdowns over the matter and was headed toward a third. My heart went out to her and I always treated her with kindness so as not to cause her more pain than she was already experiencing.

What was that "liquid light laser?" In my studies, I had read a book entitled, "The Medicine Cards" by Jamie Sams. The book and set of cards were a study of animal spirit power, or totems, the qualities some of the animals in the Native American spiritual traditions possessed and how to learn which animals are working with us. When I was working at a bar giving sample Tarot readings, the owner showed me the book and card set. Tarot readings were slow so the woman loaned me the set to occupy my time while I waited for people to arrive after work. I asked for Guidance to help me choose the correct animals for this reading and it was an amazing experience. One of the animals that appeared was Skunk. The liquid laser light shooting over my right shoulder into this secretary's eye was Skunk Medicine. I did not have to do anything. Skunk squirted the "liquid" into her eye and I thought it amazing that she attributed the dirt in her eye to me! Skunks in the wild are protected merely by their reputation. They do not need aggression or violence, no need to fight; they simply turn around with tail held high and, if necessary, squirt. I love Skunk as one of my totem animals! But that was the most obvious demonstration that I have seen with Skunk medicine. Skunk also works with recognition of and increase in self-respect. Much needed for someone with such low self-esteem. I later bought that book and set of cards so I could study and connect further the qualities and spirit of my power animals.

I found these office scenarios extremely stressful and difficult to handle. But according to my guides, these attorneys were similar in energy and behavior patterns to my parents and brought up my issues around handling authority figures, the reason why I needed to go back to work in the office. It would be nearly impossible to work through these types of issues working as a Yoga instructor full-time. Darn. But I did my best in the office and re-claimed bits of power, responsibility and higher consciousness a little at a time.

It was interesting too the impact this cleansing of consciousness had on my body. I began to experience pain in my whole body. I could hardly get out of bed in the morning to go to work downtown. Everything ached and practicing Yoga was increasingly difficult, nearly impossible. Merishkan seemed to discount this pain as over complaining or over sensitivity. Morning after morning I would get up slowly with pain piercing everywhere—this was something out of the ordinary. Then he hurt his back and for a short time had trouble getting up in the morning. He gained insight into what I was experiencing and softened with greater support. He told me that I was releasing *"bone level negativity"* and it would eventually pass. I remember enduring the pain for at least two years. What had I gotten myself into?

# 10 GETTING DOWN TO THE NITTY GRITTY – FACING PAST PAIN

At this time, I was still working in the office, practicing Yoga and meditating as much as I could. I learned about the chakras and how to cleanse and work with them. At that time, I used Shirley MacLaine's cassette tapes and video entitled "Going Within." During one solitary meditation I chose to work with a green candle. I remember drawing the green – color of healing and the heart chakra – into my heart center. I enthusiastically sucked that green color into my heart center (located at the level of the sternum) and spun it all around inside. The next day, my chest was quite sore around the area as though I had used muscles that lie dormant for a long time. The chakras are connected more with energy, our emotions and psychic sensitivities but working so diligently to cleanse and heal my heart chakra, the dross or "psychic dust" made its way into the physical for further cleansing. This would be the start of deepening compassion. I had a long way to go.

My spirit guides wasted no time getting started with healing habitual patterns. There was an incident at the house. My friend that lived upstairs and shares the same birthday misunderstood something I said or did and became angry with me. She left the house in a huff, raced backing out the driveway and squealed the tires of her car down the street. I was beside myself and went to Merishkan. I told him through sobs what happened and he told me this was a script learned in my relationship with my parents. My father in particular abandoned me for my mother when she threatened to leave him due to his and my spiritual bond. Merishkan said it was an "abandonment issue" and was calm and patient with me. As I reflect on the scenario, it is obvious my reaction far outweighed the situation. I was terrified my friend was going to "leave me," which she did for a while when she left in the car, but she had no idea what issue she triggered off in me. However, there was another lifetime contributing to this script. It unfolded when the guides instructed me to take Merishkan into "past-life regression." They said it would be productive for both of us as Merishkan had incarnated (in an extraterrestrial form, he never incarnated as Human).

In the life to which we regressed, I lived on another planet, perhaps Andromeda or on one of the stars of the Pleiades – I had blue skin. I remember this (note this was before the production of the movie Avatar) and I remember Merishkan arriving in his own inimitable way, crashing his starship. I was a young woman when I found him lying injured near a cave. He was about 6'4" tall, had the head, ears and snout like a wolf and blonde fur covering his entire body. His legs had two "knees" and he had claws instead of fingers. I was humanoid. After I found him, I ran to the village healer and beckoned her for help. She healed Merishkan and visiting him nearly every day, I subsequently fell in love with him. Some would have considered him ugly or frightening to look at, but I could feel his wisdom and maturity and he was incredibly gracious and gentlemanly. Once he was healed from his crash injuries, we continued to see each other, meeting near the cave. He fell in love with me, too. He had to be careful in touching me because his fur was ensconced in acid that would burn me if it made contact with my skin, and his claws were sharp. He covered his "hands" with cloth so we could at least hold hands. Quite the romance!

Merishkan repaired his starship, a crystalline craft shaped like a wedge of pie that connected with him telepathically when he wore his armband. He was ready to return to his planet and wanted to take me with him. I wanted to be with him. He went to my parents and the town council asking for my hand in marriage and all said "No! " Merishkan needed to get back to his planet as he was a leader there but he would not override the decision that had been made at that time. We made a pact that he would leave my planet and return to see me as often as he could. I would wait until he returned. After his last visit, I waited... and waited... Even though we had a telepathic connection, there was no word from him. A year went by, and another. Still, there was no communication. I became depressed as my parents were trying to force me to marry someone I didn't like, much less love. I was wearing down with the lack of communication and missing Merishkan. After several years with no contact, I finally acquiesced. At my parent's arrangement, I married the man they intended for me. He was cruel and raped me; I bore his children. I became despondent and did not have the strength of will to fight my parents or the man I married. During the regression, I experienced pain physically from my memory of the rape, but facing the issues allowed me to heal. Here is what happened to promote healing, once I tapped into the rest of the story.

Finally, six years after Merishkan had abruptly disappeared, he returned. He returned! When I snuck away and met him at the cave, he told me how he had been taken as a prisoner of war and was kept in a specially designed room that cut him off from any telepathic communication with anyone. He had been drugged for interrogation purposes and was tortured. His captors sterilized him as a part of their torture so he would never be able to reproduce. He felt this pain again during the regression, both the physical pain and the mental anguish. But, he had escaped his captors and returned to honor our pact to be together. I was in a place of powerlessness and depression from the marriage and being subdued by my own captors, my parents and husband. But I started to rejuvenate at the sight of him. Merishkan once again went to my parents and asked that I be allowed to leave with him. No. He went to the town council and asked again if I could leave with him. No.

Suddenly Merishkan simply picked me up and carried me away! (This is the part I love!) After he whisked me back to his crystalline starship and placed me on a lounge seat, he went to the control panel and began to lift the ship off the planet. Then he came over to me. I was still lost in the thick fog of despondency and barely coherent, but his love and presence were very healing and I began to energize. He spoke to me but I was still dazed from the past several years of sadness and depression. He took me to a planet where I could live while he worked among the stars and always, always returned. The feelings of relief, love and peace and the dreamy tone of romance always return when I focus into Merishkan coming back for me. With this kind of history together, lifetime after lifetime, it is no small wonder that I experienced feelings when I met him in meditation in this life! While he was here, we watched the series on TV "Beauty and the Beast" because we could identify with the characters so well. The guides recommended we repeat this particular regression due to the depth of the abandonment script - and we did.

Merishkan and I conducted other past-life regressions and role playing, even including Julie, at the recommendation of the guides. They said to imagine Merishkan was my prisoner to bring out his, my own or all three of our aggressions held from who-knows-what in other lifestreams; for me certainly, aggressions felt around my childhood. The guides channeled through, several of them rotating in and out to explain and offer further guidance. They told me that in another life I was a college professor that had high regard for the intellect but devalued emotions and connection to others. He became totally withdrawn from society, taught college classes and remained in his ivory tower. He had vast knowledge and traveled all over the world, but his emotional body was closed down and out of balance. At the age of 42, he went mad and died. My guides explained that when this depth of trauma exists in a nearby life (perceiving time from more of a linear perspective as opposed to the simultaneous time perspective), one must become very aware in a clean-up life such as this incarnation for 4 years before the age of death/trauma and for 4 years after in order to break the pattern. They explained that I would need to become very aware during this time because the professor life could draw me back into the pattern, and that I had chosen a similar personality in this life and could be drawn down the same path to madness. They said it is called "bleed-through" when we are open to other lifestreams and they spill into the current life, like this one. (Usually we set up memory blocks at birth so that we are not distracted by other lifestreams allowing us to fully focus in this lifetime, but in a clean-up life, it is sometimes necessary to access those memories to heal the wounds and traumas.) During the time Merishkan was here and the guides were channeling, I was 40 years old. The professor life heavily impacted me in the way I related with people in this life. I was unaware, but friends told me I would not let anyone get close to me and like my professor counterpart, I felt little if any connectedness. I would even leave the room where a channeling session was being conducted or during a party without saying a word to anyone—just left. I ignored my feelings, though I had felt a sense of angst all my life to this point, I expressed very little. Even in the psychic development class Merishkan was teaching, I could lay my hands on someone and psychically see their skeleton, like an x-ray, as I moved my hands along their body. But I did not feel anything, even though I was naturally empathic I lacked awareness or sufficient self-esteem to handle it. Consciously, I allowed very little feeling. Merishkan drew out love from me as he gave freely, so I was learning to recognize it and to some degree, trust.

To heal from this impactful lifestream, I recognized that my childhood reinforced this pattern. I believe part of the reason I chose this treatment from family, especially my mother, was in order to bring catharsis to heal the professor life. *As a matter of fact, the guides told me it was a spiritual agreement because if my mother had not treated me like she did in this lifetime, I would not have felt compelled to plummet the depths of my psyche, unearthing all the issues and pain I needed to recognize and neutralize this time around.* They said it would be my next life that I would have abilities similar to Paramahansa Yogananda and that even he went through this type of purging (known as the fires of purification). All must go through this stage of clearing.

I began meditations with this professor self and felt him pulling me into that life. The patterns here were intensifying as I continued to withdraw from people. Until Merishkan arrived I had few friends and socialized very little. I had always been quiet and introverted and now I was being drawn in to deeper darkness. In meditation, I told my professor self that I wanted him to stay in that life and quit trying to suck energy from me in this life. I told him I wanted to learn to relate with people, to love and be loved. I had to draw a curtain on him to distinguish between lives. This was very real and serious. The guides triggered my recognition when they spoke of the professor life and I came to recognize the patterns. This would be very similar to one of your parents reminding you of something that happened to you as a child that was filed in your long-term memory—then with recognition, you say, ah-ha!    I remember that! And further memory unfolds.   The meditations were effective and after a while I no longer felt the pull to withdraw from people so much. This particular subconscious patterning was melting in the Light of awareness. Later on, I sent love to this professor fellow with huge doses of compassion. What a sad life he led.

I believe though when we reach a certain level of evolution or enlightenment in one life, it emits that enlightenment into our other lives and heals all of them. Time is simultaneous, all of our lives are occurring at the same time. Much like the mirrors on a disco ball each segment represents an individual life. All are happening at once as our Higher Self, connected to the Source/Creator, channels into each and every life. We all channel.

Merishkan and the guides taught me too about "alternate realities" or "alternate probability lines." This is related somewhat to other lifetimes or lifestreams. When in an incarnation we face a difficult choice, when we are at a crossroads and make a decision, we see the results of our choice in this physical dimension, this state of awareness. But another part of us made a different choice and we can connect with the part of us that made another choice. Here is an example of one I experienced spontaneously while working in the law firm. I had asked for the experience and Spirit granted my request.

If you recall the story where I was six years old and my parents and we three kids stood on the sidewalk in town just having attended a Methodist church service. Mom and Dad were arguing because Mom wanted the whole family to attend the Baptist Church and Dad wanted to attend the Methodist Church. We kids were caught in the middle without a vote. Mom won and the die was cast:  we would all attend the Baptist Church. Back then, this church was based on fear and this was the church where the head deacon had an affair with my mother and molested me. My inner creative child knew when my parents walked down the aisle "to be saved" that she would die here, she was already dying from the family dynamic and this would clinch the deal. She split off from me at that point taking the greater portion of my creativity with her. Later on she returned, but here is how another choice showed itself.

I was working in a downtown Cleveland law firm in the mid-1980's while Merishkan and the guides were here and I was healing a lot of issues. The firm's offices spanned several floors and we could avoid waiting at the elevator by taking the internal stairs. One day I was on those stairs and I spontaneously felt "me" at age 13 come into my awareness. This was the "me" that had chosen other than the Baptist Church. She felt free and filled with joy and lightheartedness. She had not been taught she was born in sin and hence faulty from birth. She had not been manipulated with fear of going to hell if she broke any of the rules and restrictions of the fundamentalist belief system of that time, in a small town. I assimilated her energy. She felt so free within me, happy and light. I could feel her uninhibited, childlike innocence and confidence that was maturing into the wisdom of a young woman. I could feel her <u>POWER</u>. This was an opportunity, as strange as it may seem, to let go of some of the conditioning I received in my childhood.

I understand that not all churches of this denomination operated this way or had this effect on people, and perhaps having been born into an alcoholic family dynamic exacerbated my issues. But for me, any church or paradigm that does not allow for the psycho-spiritual aspect and personal guidance system or intuition cannot work for me. While doing laundry at the Laundromat, I talked with a seminary student in Ashland, OH who had been a counselor for many years. He told me the highest percentage of his clients or patients were there to de-program and debrief from certain protestant teachings that bordered on brainwashing. My guides that channeled through told me I could have chosen compassion as a Baptist child, but under the circumstances, I was filled with fear and hate already and I do not believe I had sufficient exposure to compassion then to internalize it as a way of being. Years later, in the early 1990's, during a meditation at Christmas time, I once again had a vision with Jesus. In this vision, Jesus had not been crucified and killed, he was well loved and he spread that love and compassion everywhere he went. I have read two other accounts of this same awareness and I will trust my intuition over any indoctrination that is out there. Perhaps those in power during the inquisition and witch burnings are the same ones that distorted biblical writings and reality working to disempower people by showing the need for sacrifice and salvation as a means of mass control. I do not push my beliefs on anyone, but I also do not allow theirs to be pushed onto me. "Witch" brings me to another lifestream on the agenda for healing (pun intended).

During a private Yoga session I was giving to a friend, we came to the end of the class where the student lies in the Corpse Pose or Relaxation Pose (Savasana) to allow deep relaxation and homeostasis. While my friend relaxed, I went into meditation. I did not ask for any vision nor did I have any expectation. But in the vision came. I saw myself being burned at the stake, watching my face in grimace as the flames lapped at my legs and torso. My arms were bound behind my back securing me to the post positioned on top of pile of flaming branches. I was simply observing this event, with no sense of pain, but I knew I was the woman and I was being burned as a Witch. This vision was like an introduction, opening me to the memory of the traumatic event and the need for healing the emotions around it. I remembered more as I looked up Joan of Arc, torture and so forth in the "Women's Encyclopedia of Myths and Secrets," a thick and scholarly book authored by Barbara Walker. As I read, I could feel the sensations in my body. As I read about the clamps placed on a woman's legs and squeezing to torture her, I could feel it in my own legs. I could tell by the sensations in my body where the tortures had occurred.

I soon noticed something else. Merishkan had a very close bond with one of the guides that channeled through him. He was called "Produce" since he was vegetarian in his most recent human incarnation and was a biker. He was heading for California when he was involved in an accident that caused him to be decapitated. Most of the time Merishkan and I saw pretty much eye-to-eye, but I did not feel the same sense of closeness with Produce and I wondered why. He was amusing, spiritual and provided non-judgmental, comic relief at times when the issues we were facing were intense and painful. I pondered the question as to why I did not feel the same camaraderie with Produce. Then it occurred to me. I had an intuitive flash where I simply knew Produce was one of my inquisitors in the life where I was burned at the stake. This answer rang true and I felt it was right within my body. I never mentioned any of this to Merishkan or anyone, but soon thereafter Produce channeled through to confirm my memory. (Yes, they can hear our thoughts!) He said he had gone back to that lifestream with one of his own guides and they reviewed the events (a life review). He was not happy with what he observed. I also learned that we assess ourselves when we are ready to review each lifestream—there is no "judgment day," though the "day of reckoning" is similar in that we must eventually accept responsibility for the ramifications of our actions and thoughts (karma). But there is no judge other than ourselves that evaluates us as only we know our own feelings and readiness to heal and face the Truth. A guardian or guide always accompanies us to provide support in the process.

Produce channeled and confirmed that he was my inquisitor and that he was one of those that tortured me. Around this time, Produce had the opportunity to leave our circle of friends to go make plans for his upcoming incarnation, but he chose to stay and work with us. This allowed him to "balance his karma," to neutralize the pattern he developed as an inquisitor and to release himself from the chains of grief and sorrow over his participation in those events. He was helping in channel to teach, bring through information and love and help us grow spiritually. He would move on to make his next incarnational plans when the channeling and walk-in situation came to a close.

My own healing of that Witch life came in a most interesting way. A cosmic set-up was arranged when I offered a prayer for the healing of the fear, anger and oppression I held within my body over that experience. I was working in a large, world-wide headquarters of a law firm that occupied several floors in a building in downtown Cleveland. It was the same day around Thanksgiving, November 20, 1992, when there was a fire at Windsor Castle in England. Coincidentally, our firm was scheduled for a fire drill that day and I felt a twinge of intuition that this would be "healing day." We were located on floors 42 through 49 so instead of a full mass exodus, we were only required to walk down three flights of stairs, wait for the okay to return to our individual floors and take the elevators back up. There were hall monitors wearing red hats at the entrances to the internal stairwells and the alarm for the drill sounded. I walked alone toward one of the red-hats and could feel the fear welling up inside of me. I felt strange and knew something unusual was about to happen. People were laughing and poking fun at each other as we descended the internal stairs. The fear grew in my solar plexus. I began to feel I was walking in both worlds, this one in the office fire drill, and the other, the Witch life where I was being escorted to be burned at the stake. The people that were laughing and jeering in the stairwell represented those laughing and jeering at me as a defeated Witch walking the final steps of my journey. I felt tears and anger fill my throat and yet I felt a sense of surrender as there was nowhere to turn. All the employees from our floor arrived at the assigned destination and the drill was over. We were allowed to return to our desks by way of the elevator. I was still feeling both worlds unfolding before me. The elevator I entered was full to capacity and as the door opened on the other floors with more employees hoping to enter, some of the attorneys laughed at them saying, "Burn, baby, burn! " They were joking of course, but I was also hearing it from the other side of the veil where it was meant for me. At this point, I could feel a huge ball of uncomfortable energy in my solar plexus welling up even more and emotions vying for release. I felt frantic and wanted to cry. I tried calling a friend that might have understood, but her line was busy and I could not reach her. I nearly staggered to the ladies' room and took my chances with whoever might be there. I began to sob vehemently. I felt as though I was vomiting a huge ball of emotion from my belly and then I noticed an attorney leaving the stall and another woman, an acquaintance, who appeared compassionate. I merely stated the fire drill brought back a horrible memory and I needed to release. I felt myself in catharsis, shaking and temporarily drained by the experience, but I released that stuck energy and felt greatly relieved.

Upon returning to my desk, I could perceive the warm, thick yellow glow of Light that I have seen before during catharsis. The entire room appeared to be permeated with this golden glow and I noticed how everyone, attorneys and staff alike, were treating me with compassion the remainder of that afternoon. This was not the usual scenario in a busy, demanding law firm. My workload was light the rest of the day too, allowing me time to integrate my experience and gain equilibrium. I had experienced the fear, terror and hopelessness of myself as a Witch in that life—the karma was neutralized and I felt peaceful.

Even though this healing was written a little out of time sequence, I felt it would be a better flow for you reading about the issue all at once rather than in actual time sequence. Many things transpired before this cosmic set-up so I will go back to mid-1980 where Merishkan, the other angels and the whole entourage are engaged in channeling and teaching.

# 11 HOW DID I GET SO FEARFUL?

I posed this question to Merishkan and we sat down with the Tarot cards. I made notes of the information and answers that came through. It was a profound session as Merishkan was a profound being. The date was August 7, 1988. I will record the information here. I suspect that if I received the programming and scripts I have recorded here, then a lot of other people may have too. Some of these answers may apply somehow for you, if not, disregard them or see if they are applicable for a friend, a child, a loved one.

How Did I Get So Fearful?

### 1st position, Princess of Cups

My challenges came with my non-socialized self and my naturally psychic self together. These two aspects could not work in harmony, thus I could trust no one, not even myself or God. I learned hopelessness through thwarted and repressed spontaneity. In my spiritual body, my relationship to God, I was in constant fear of being spanked; I learned God was an avenging, punishing God rather than loving and nurturing. As a little girl, I refused to sleep without a sheet at night for fear God would spank me. My nature is to need people and to nurture them. Also to revel in sharing love with others, but I closed down these natural tendencies, nipped them in the bud. I learned powerlessness and was unable to rely on myself. I had no control over my life – this brought deeply penetrating fear.

### 2nd position, Five of Cups

My twin brother and I were not taught how to communicate so the alternative was isolation. In the Sun card for example, we twins reach out to each other and there is a wall to protect us, representing limitations, clear and well defined rules. In this, the Five of Cups, we have our backs to each other, unable to communicate. The wall is ambiguous, the rules we had kept us in fear. We never knew what would displease our mother. What was okay one day was forbidden another day and would get us grounded a third day, and so on. There was no consistency, which to a kid is security. We had to constantly walk on egg shells. We had no guidelines, clearly defined codes for communicating. The ambiguity played out in conversation between us twins: What did we do wrong? I don't know, what do you think we did wrong? I don't know. And so on.

### 3rd position, Two of Swords

We were taught we were incapable of making decisions for ourselves, but also we had to make choices or decisions and it had to be the right one. To make a mistake is a major disaster. On one hand, we cannot make decisions but if we do, it had better be the right one, and this, without being taught how to make a decision. Also we were not able to turn to others for help in making decisions. My ex-husband also contributed in the script that I could not make a decision for myself or ask for help. I was not to be independent enough to make some decisions but must stay dependent enough on him to build his ego.

### 4th position (opportunity), High Priestess

My intuition, my innate psychicism, past-life memories, ability to communicate with guides are normally a strength/talent, but also in this position means social consciousness. I was taught to deny my own intuition and instead turn to the church or mother for answers. Listening to my inner voice or feelings on an issue was wrong—it could be the devil tempting me. Don't listen to self – do what mother tells me. Mother is always right, even though mother contradicts herself every day. Don't listen to gut feelings, don't say what you know to be true (i.e., Me: "Daddy, you're neurotic according to this article." Mom: "Shush! Don't say that!") Don't listen to my own feelings. Trust authorities even though authorities abuse that trust. (Isn't this happening to most of us all over the world, even now in 2014? We all need to claim our power.)

I also learned that to turn to someone else for answers or insight means to automatically squelch my own intuition or stop my own psychicism. It happens with me turning to Merishkan for answers but subconscious programming says to shut down my own psychic gifts. As a kid, I turned to mother for answers and did not listen for my own gut feelings. And when someone else is right, I am not valid. With the deacon's behavior, his being an authority figure for me both spiritually and personally, when he misbehaved, it was not that he was wrong, it threw me into confusion. If I had been permitted my own intuition, it would have been simply, he is wrong! Plus throw in a little betrayal, but no confusion. I was taught to be cut off from my intuition and that grown-ups are always right, even if I'm getting screwed. This created more fear. (Other women treated like this?)

### 5ᵗʰ position, Strength Card

I learned to not trust my body. Be spineless, with no backbone, therefore develop weak spine (twin brother and me). I came close to needing back surgery like brother. Also, whole family was taught illness as a way of being. I learned from Mother to always be sick and always tired. We had to try and fulfill contradictory messages. Subconsciously we will try to keep all of the programs happy and try to meet the needs of all the messages. I had the message of "I hate to sleep in" because of being forced to stay in bed on Saturday mornings as a child – be quiet for Mother - but also got message that the way to escape an intolerable situation is to sleep. So, I learned contradicting messages and had to fulfill all of them. On one hand, sleep more when the going gets tough, but on the other hand, have to stay awake in order to accomplish things. I hated to sleep in anyway because that is one way mother abused me.

### 6ᵗʰ position, Center, essential self, sense of self/core of situation– Eight of Cups

Loss and spilled cups – self-sabotage. I learned no matter what I accomplished, no matter what cups I filled, I had to kick them over. Cups could represent wealth but I don't deserve wealth and it's bad anyway. Subconscious message was I must sabotage any accomplishments. Good way to cause fear. There was no sense of security - according to the church, to exhibit any power is not good. "Blessed are the meek," blessed is the victim. Actually, "meek" should equal "happy go lucky". Blessed are those who fulfill the qualities of the Fool card! (Happy go lucky) Confusion comes from following King James Version – is mangled, distorted. Study your Bible but don't try to think for yourself what it means. Interpret it as you are taught to interpret it. Derive conclusions learned from my own church. Sabotage any gains, don't show power, act inferior in order to boost husband's (or others') ego. "Don't boost someone's ego by helping them heal—boost someone's ego by acting inferior." (Blink, blink, blink! ) Sabotage any of my own power I was struggling to develop. I abandoned my job at one office – in part – to sabotage and undermine gains and career advancement.

### 7ᵗʰ position, Princess of Wands

My sister was bigger and my twin brother and I had no leverage to fight her. The two of us combined could not overcome her. We had no examples of unity. Two people uniting against a common foe—how would we have known? We never saw it. Also, we had no communication skills.

### 8th position, World Card

Non-acceptance of body – my sexuality/sensuality was deemed not good, not valid. I was a naturally sensual/physical person. I was taught flesh is evil, female flesh is even worse.

### 9th position, Knight of Pentacles

This card in this position refers to normal childhood fears, i.e., boogey man under the bed, beast in the closet, etc. Childhood terrors of the imagination are normal and typical. Most of the time these fears are fairly manageable but we had so many fears already that normal fears were overload. Generally a child can come up with his own remedies for ways of keeping the creature in the closet at bay. Certain stuffed animals will protect, for example. But we already had so much to deal with, it was just too much. Also, fears around being my twin's protector on top of this caused more stress. *But this gave me a seed of power* when I had no sense of power. What I could not do for myself, I found the ability to do for him. He needed me. So I felt power where I never would have succeeded in finding it for myself. This was probably an agreement we made before the incarnation. It gave me something I could connect with once I began connecting with myself and healing myself.

### 10th position, Five of Swords

I learned defeat and betrayal are what the world is about, which also instills fear. I was taught the world is like the Five of Swords—those closest to me will betray me and will not love me.

### 11th position, Justice

I point out to people where they are in harmony with Natural Law. For instance, teaching my ex-husband that this is healthy, that is not. This is in accord with Natural Law, and that is not, etc. This scenario is providing vindication for my inner child. Now I'm telling those people that held me back what to do. This is appeasing my inner child. Ex-husband is going through scenario similar to our divorce only he is now in my position and feeling what it is like to be treated unfairly. He is going through the exact parallel and I'm able to watch but also counsel him through it. My Justice prayers are coming around. Part of justice is being there to observe his situation so my inner child can feel justice has been done – she needs that "there, I told you so," and "a taste of your own medicine," etc. *This represents a legitimate need for vindication, and is not malicious. For all that we're taught that vengeance is not spiritual, it is a legitimate need for the inner child to be vindicated in whatever way possible.* It represents a wish for things to be fair or balanced karma. So I was a participant while he went through a re-enactment of what my inner child felt was not a fairly handled divorce. She felt I got screwed both in marriage and divorce. There was not a balance between what he gave me and what he took from me, both during and after marriage. This is a way for my inner child to get the odds evened out. I'm there to say, "There, I told you so, here's what you did." And I'm there to help him. *This is part of a judicial agreement sent down by the Goddess.* He goes through it again, in front of my nose so I can feel it is now fair and also I will help him heal through it. Justice card in the outcome represents "Let Justice be done" prayers paying off, so a lot of old inequities and fears can be balanced out. Where it is not possible to do it with the original people, I am doing dramatizations. With my ex, I'm doing it with another woman in my place. With my parents, because I cannot work directly with them, I am being an assistant to a Yoga student named Shelley to dramatize that she represents me as a child and receives my help. Helping her is the same as helping myself as a child since she has parents similar to mine. With her, I am the assistant I wished I had as a kid. To my inner child, that makes things even. Shelley represents a younger me/Michelle. No coincidence in the similarity between our names. The 6 of Pentacles shows up here, in personal power position where fear has disrupted the flow of my own power and ability to communicate. I am balancing things out.

## 12th position, Knight of Swords (2nd chakra position)

The work Merishkan and I are doing with regressions is helping me to burst through aggression and violence in others. In regressions, Merishkan shows me parts of me and my family that I could not handle and gives me a foundation in which I can be in control of what my inner child perceives are very uncontrollable and unpredictable situations. These regressions give me control over something I felt I could not control. I am punching through past-life experiences as well. Some of the regressions might be frightening because I am being faced with points where I was with Merishkan when he was out of control.

In addition to this healing reading, the guides channeled through and presented core issues which may be common to others as well as me. In the interest of sharing, I am presenting this material for your consideration and reflection just as the guides presented it to me.

Programming: Male side danger is complacency and indifference to others. Male = contentment and solitude. They said I don't know what a woman is.

The female in me is a source of discipline – women put pressure on me to be who I am not, instead of giving me the traditions.

Core Issue: Women can't ever be happy and secure alone; male side is happy only alone.

1. To be happy one must fulfill male solitariness and insensitive to needs of others – man is oblivious – woman will sabotage it. Divide and conquer.

2. Man is complete until woman comes along; woman isn't complete until a man comes along.

3. Woman will sabotage man's freedom and individuality.

4. Woman will sabotage her family (abuse)

5. Woman will sabotage her success in business world; only way is to be individualist in workplace where team spirit is called for. (Group activity is by definition female – so, unhappy).

6 She will sabotage her creative self (success) because by definition women cannot be complete unless part of man.

7. Will sabotage relationships – he will ignore her and be indifferent to her needs – men are inaccessible. (She won't assert her own needs, would break man's obliviousness.) Julie embodied all of this.

8. Has letter of the law but not spirit of the law – follows all the rules but still isn't happy.

9. Women are never healthy – must sabotage good health or any advances made, including job.

10. Confusion over emotions – "hold them in but don't;" also rollercoaster.

11. I learned that *love and violence are inseparable* – to love someone is to in some way destroy them. Misogynist – foundation and self-sabotage. I apply this everywhere: destroy before am destroyed.

12. Belief in hardship and poverty.

Moon = understanding feminine mysteries.

Exercise:  define 5 ways mother was happy during my childhood and adolescence
1. emotional (relationship)
2. physical – out in the world – body and environment
3. creative will – assertion of self and power
4. communication and intellect (mind); knowledge and ability to communicate it.
5. spiritual

Is there anything healthy I can keep?

Affirmations:  let them be rooted in actions. Affirm what I want to be. How do I see fulfillment in those 5 areas?

Selective truth:  black and white; good and bad

SOLUTION:  look at reality, ideal and negative programming. What can be done to balance discrepancy?

These were all the challenges I took on at my level of soul growth. I have progressed to this level of challenge. When we reach a certain point, we are required to take certain classes. *Challenges and obstacles I encounter on the path are inherent in the path I have chosen.* That's the game we're all playing. But wait, there's more!

Merishkan also told me to try this technique to tap into fear: he said to go into meditation and ask that my fear be shown as the biggest, ugliest, slimiest, gross-est, meanest and darkest monster I could imagine. Then I was to ask it to come around in front of me where I could see it. I was to send it feelings of love and compassion and wait to see what happens. So after my next Yoga practice session, I sat down and followed his instructions.

I sat on the floor in front of my altar preparing for meditation. I practiced deep breathing for a few rounds and descended into a relaxed, altered state. I created a mental picture of the biggest, darkest, meanest, ugliest and slimiest glob of a monster I could summon. Then I could feel it behind me to my right. I asked it to come around in front of me where I could see it. It waddled, ambling around in front of me, a massive lump of black, shiny with slime, and ugly. Instead of feeling it was mean and aggressive, I felt humility in the creature, and immense sadness. I was soon overcome with compassion for this beast and felt a strong urge to send it love in the form of a mental hug. Suddenly the monster magically transformed into an entity appearing on the floor in the right front corner of the room. I realized it was a child, a little girl, quaking and shuddering, knees drawn to her chest, arms inside her thighs. She sat pitched against the angled walls. She was shaking in terror. I knew the child was me; she lived inside me. I had been the monster as well, disguised in the darkness of fear and masquerading through life hoping to be protected by the illusion represented by the "monster." Continuing with my meditation, I walked over to the little girl and scooped her up in my arms to bring her Home with me, to integrate her energy into mine.

As I became more consciously aware of what happened to me as a child and the resulting damage, I also became aware of how I was filled with rage. When I vacuumed the carpet, I became a "rage-aholic" and did not even recognize it until this point. In talking with Merishkan and the guides channeling through, it was suggested, since I was not yet confident enough to discuss with my family, that I write them a letter. They suggested that I write my feelings but not in a venting way. I wrote to my mother expressing how I felt angry and disappointed at how she treated me and about some specific things she did to make me feel that way. She wrote back and denied everything with which I confronted her. I did not keep either of our letters, but realize now I should not have expected anything other than the response I received. My family did not like Merishkan (who they thought was Coyote, publicly we addressed him/her as Coyote) and they felt s/he was in league with the devil and was pulling me in that direction too. If they only knew!

My mother and sister invited me to a Tupperware party but refused to allow Merishkan to come, so I declined. I became estranged from my family for the next two years, refusing little, if any, contact with them. From then on, I steered clear of family. I needed to work through these emotions and memories without any further pull from them. It was a very confusing time, sorting out the religious dogma, abuse, integrating my new truths, the emotional and family drama, the emotions that were unleashed and needed acknowledgement while still working a full-time job in a place where my familial abuses were being re-enacted through my bosses. Our work continued. Julie at times felt intimidated and found it mind-boggling the speed in working through issues that Merishkan and I exhibited. We could handle several issues at a time where she preferred to work with one at a time. We choose what we set up for ourselves in pre-incarnation planning. Let me interject here, Rob Schwartz has two wonderful books published, *Your Soul's Plan* and *Your Soul's Gift* that detail the creation of these plans and how they are played out during the incarnation. Young Michelle needed attention and I intended to provide it for her.

# 12 THE GOODNESS OF MERISHKAN... AND OTHERS (SURPRISE!)

Merishkan, the angels and assorted human and non-human entities that channeled through him, including Gaia and Goddess Kali, were all supportive through this whole re-integration process. Produce brought comic relief and the others brought through emphasis on love, forgiveness, compassion and balance. Even my Yogi Spirit Guide named Ashero who said his bones were long ago buried in India channeled through advising Julie and me what poses to work on for whatever issues we were facing. Ashero used standard spirit guide techniques and gained my trust through humor and then slipped in a pearl of wisdom to chip away at my ego. He channeled a few times and then announced he would not channel again until he channeled through me. I had dreams with him where he was helping me with Yoga poses. Sometimes I would play with him during Yoga practice, getting into a pose and asking him to keep me from falling, like in a handstand. He played along and I didn't fall.

Merishkan's patience through it all was commensurate with his angelic nature. He is a silver angel, often called a "dark" angel. White angels bring order with their presence, dark angels (silver, like mercury or a piece of hematite) bring chaos and stir things up so the issues can be addressed and healed, also to inspire creativity. Note that there are other colors of angels as well, I've seen red ones and green ones, there's purpose in all. He would drop into channel at the most ridiculous of our questions and was most of the time charming and accommodating. He had the rare adeptness to be able to "cannonball" down into deep trance, to zoom down and channel information accurately. There were times when he was working through his own issues that he would pull back to integrate for himself. He came to this walk-in scenario under the energy of Scorpio and Scorpios are often intense and need to dig deep for transformation to find the Light. He would go into a bit of a blue funk for a few days until he had sorted things out and was just a little less social during those times. He was so compassionate and fair; everyone loved him, though everyone but Julie and I thought Merishkan was Coyote. The love grew amongst our little family and I relished the thought of spending my life with Merishkan. Through Merishkan's commitment, Coyote's cooperation and the host of angels and entities channeling through him, we had the most conducive arena possible to work on our excavation.

When Merishkan smiled, he didn't just smile with his mouth, he smiled with his eyes, and they twinkled. The guides explained that it takes "a whopper" of a consciousness and energy force to "walk in" as Merishkan did. And the Brotherhood of Light, a council of angels overseeing the activities on Earth and offering protection to us in order that the best and highest good can have opportunity to play out within our free will choice, had to approve any and all walk-in situations. Produce wanted to come in as a walk-in so he could be with someone he dearly loved here, but he was not yet evolved sufficiently to pull it off. The Brotherhood denied his request. There are always walk-ins all over the planet that come into someone else's body, someone that no longer wants to be here and the entity walking in wants to avoid the diaper stage, but the walk-ins that came during this time were here for a special purpose. That will be revealed later.

Over a period of years, Merishkan channeled the Goddess Kali (known well in India, a Goddess with whom I have worked in other incarnations when I incarnated in India and served as a guru), many angels, Gaia and other enlightened humans not only for me, but also for guests who came to our home to listen during his channeling sessions. He (in Coyote's body and with her voice, of course) was on the Morning Exchange and The John Lannigan Radio Show. I still have the cassette tape of this interview. He had the option, but ultimately made the decision to circumvent the celebrity route for personal reasons. There were other walk-ins on the Earth that did become celebrities, but it is not widely known who they are.

The guides wanted Merishkan to take Yoga with me, but it brought up powerful emotions and he was too private for that. In the alternative, the guides then recommended we do another regression with him. There are those that say there was no "angel rebellion," but here is what Merishkan revealed during that regression. I saw it too, receiving visuals through his description of the events. Whether it was an actual event in truth or an alternate probability line, Merishkan experienced it and was still impacted by the losses he suffered.

Merishkan was still carrying pain from what the guides called "the angel rebellion." Merishkan explained that once the Human Race was created, the angels were given dominion over us. They were at odds around deciding whether or not we should have free will choice. Apparently no other species had been blessed with free will and the angels were widely divided on the issue. Obviously we have free will, so we know who won the argument, but Merishkan's regression allowed me to see through his eyes the scenario as it played out. Here is how it unfolded.

Lucifer (also a silver or "dark" angel) was the leader of the faction of angels who wished for us to have free will, and Merishkan was a part of it too. The two factions went to war over the issue, those that felt strongly the newly created Human Race should have free will choice, and those that felt we should not be allowed free will. I could see the fight visually on the screen of my mind as we worked together in the regression. All the angels were armed with laser lights for swords; there was a light show of laser beams flashing everywhere as they fought. (This story imparts new meaning to the term, "as above, so below.") Lucifer's group finally won the battle, but many angels died. Merishkan explained that when an angel is killed, his energy is dispersed out into the Universe, never to be combined again, the individual is lost forever. When a Human is killed or dispersed, the soul's energy recombines and congeals. Merishkan lost many dear friends in that war and was still grieving at this time.

Merishkan further revealed that the one condition upon which the losing side would concede free will choice to the Human Race was that the angels who fought for freedom would have to incarnate as Humans Beings or in some other incarnating race. This is what was termed the "fall" to which religious history refers. These angels "fell" into human incarnations, *lowering their vibrations* to experience firsthand the free will choice they provided for us. This was when I first met Merishkan, eons ago in one of his first incarnations though he was humanoid, not human, as I was. This was painful for Merishkan, being removed from the angelic realm and his friends to experience incarnations, though there were many angels forced to take on the Human incarnational cycle. He felt the loss of those permanently blown apart and scattered in space.

The "fall" was also the inauguration of the "bad rap" bestowed upon Lucifer, building over time into a reputation of "the devil." Lucifer actually channeled through Merishkan and clarified the story. The story demonstrates that there never was a devil but over eons of time, Human judgment and negativity have been heaped upon Lucifer for having the courage to fight for humans to have free will. I realize this story may seem a stretch to you, but if you also study <u>The Woman's Encyclopedia of Myths and Secrets</u>, by Barbara G. Walker (Harper & Row, 1983, pps. 551-554), you will see another version of history of this being besides that of the "devil."

It would seem to me that without a "devil" upon which to project judgment and negativity (in a word, blame), we humans would be forced to take responsibility for our actions and evolve. Perhaps the "devil" is actually our own weakness and accumulated negativity that builds into a force of its own. This might be a concept worthy of consideration, especially in light of my experience having the dragon-thought form removed from my head and spine which you will see described in the next chapter.

# 13 UNDER CONSTRUCTION, OR RATHER, RE-CONSTRUCTION

Working with Merishkan and his merry band of angels and other entities, was a delight, aside from the work itself being so intense. Julie and I both wanted to get through this as quickly as possible and we would whine about how long it was taking. We kept asking if we could expedite the expedition and get on with life. I will warn you now, be careful what you ask for. Once our prayers were answered and things got kicked up a notch, we *really* started whining!   When we asked the guides what was happening, they told us our prayers for a faster pace of healing were answered and this was it!

Now the process was speeded up, and it was even more of a challenge to keep up with the healing of our poor, battered egos. We learned, however, that we have a maximum psychic threshold where if we go beyond a certain point, it is detrimental to our health and wellbeing—we could go insane. We were now pressed tightly against that point, right to the edge. What were we thinking!

One evening the guides wanted Merishkan to channel since they had some sort of announcement for me. One of the angels came in and told me that once we step upon the spiritual path, there is a period of working with Spirit to heal and grow. However, after a certain amount of time on the path, where we have proven our integrity and commitment, there is a "point of no return." After this point, even if we *want* to turn back, we cannot!   We are held accountable for our decision and commitment. The angels announced to me I had reached that point. There was no turning back, ever. They told me, and I have since read during my studies, that there is no more an unhappy person than one that has committed, reached the point of no return and then given up on his spiritual path. With the amount of healing I needed to achieve, and at the pace we had whined ourselves up to, Life would be interesting to say the least.

# I Forgive You, Daddy – Yoga and the Angels Healed Me!

One day when things seemed to be going pretty well, I had a headache. My body had healed from the two-year period of intense pain (releasing "bone level negativity") and I was feeling great in my Sadhana (personal Yoga practice). But this day, I had a headache. I tried stretching and deep breathing in a Yoga practice session, I tried self-massage, visualization—I just could not get rid of this headache. Having done my best to handle it myself but without success, I asked Merishkan if he would try to help.

Merishkan walked over to where I was sitting in the dining room and placed his hands over my head. He energetically reached down into my crown chakra (the spiritual energy center we all have in the top of our heads) and with both hands pulled out a beastly creature. I could not see it, he described it afterward. It resembled a combination wolf-dragon having a large snout with lots of teeth, tall ears, was slimy, and had a long tail. Merishkan rushed to the kitchen sink and washed the energy monster down the drain, explaining that these thought-form creatures will bite and can cause injury, but also they are dissolved in water, the universal cleanser.

Within minutes my headache was completely gone. My spine felt better too, as though it was more open somehow—I could feel a new sense of space around my spine. Upon mentioning this to Merishkan, he said the tail of the creature was wrapped around my spine. I mentioned feeling sad that after so many years of practicing Yoga (15 years at this point) such a negative creature could still exist in my body and energy field. I thought I was further along on the path. Merishkan explained that all of my Yoga practice had loosened the critter's tail so it could be lifted out. He told me that the creature was a thought form created by my mother yelling and screaming in my face throughout my childhood and it had congealed into this separate entity with a budding consciousness of its own. It took a whole day for the area around my spine to fill in with White Light. I could physically feel the sensations. And my headache never came back.

Living in a home where psychic development is accepted gave me permission to open more to my own gifts and creativity. Having such a low self-image I had not yet embraced the creative part of myself. I had many lucid healing dreams and this one brought me deep insight and renewal of compassion.

In the dream, I was my adult self, walking through the forest while scrutinizing a sheet of paper that I held in both hands—it looked like 8 ½ x 11 white typing paper, nothing unusual, except for one thing. The paper was a multi-colored finger painting that I had created. Even though I was an adult, I had created a finger painting. How unsophisticated of me. As I looked at my creation, I felt utter disgust toward this childishly unrefined excuse for artwork. I crumpled the paper into a ball and threw it on the ground near the trunk of one of the trees. The tree had taproots or water roots above ground and the ball of paper landed amidst these roots. As I looked down at the scrapped paper, still feeling critically judgmental, one of the taproots began to move. As I watched, the finger-like roots slowly, laboriously stretched, reaching out, turning upward and carefully curling around the artwork litter as though it were a live child itself being held in the tree's clasp. The message conveyed telepathically to me was that the tree would hold and protect my art (creativity) until I could fully appreciate my own talents, abilities and creativity.

This dream affected me so profoundly that I wept on and off for three days. The fact that anyone, especially a non-human, would care deeply enough to offer protection for and the honoring of my creativity--even when producing something as simple and unsophisticated as a child's finger painting, created by an adult--was moving! I could barely comprehend the notion. It took many years to root out the programming that I could not do anything right or that I could not create something of value, worth or beauty (including myself). It took a while to even think of this dream without being emotionally stirred.

Notice that this dream shows not only the tree spirit's compassion, honoring my creativity when I did not, but it alludes to my reverence for the forest and spirits residing there. I have had other dreams where I walked in the woods and talked with a tree spirit that assumed the appearance of a human so that I could relate more easily. It was an interesting dream too in that in real life I would never litter in the woods as I did throwing away that paper. During the dream, I felt my observer-self gasp at the act of littering. In some of my dreams, there are evergreens all dressed up in their thick, white, wintery finery and I walk among them mesmerized by their beauty. Much healing can happen on the dream plane.

One healing dream happened while Merishkan was here. This is still in the late 1980's. I saw myself standing across from and facing a large, teddy-bear-type black man. I knew this man was my father even though he appeared differently. We hugged each other and I felt a surge of energy leaving my body and going into his—this caused him pain and suffering and he began to cry. (Realize here that my Capricorn father rarely expressed emotion.) Immediately I felt the urge to take back the energy, but it was too late. Then I realized that he had taken back all the pain and suffering he had ever caused me in our relationship. Any healing that was left was to be done on my own. He had done his part by receiving my pain on the dream plane and the rest was up to me. It was strange, though, I was not aware of what he had done to cause me that much pain.

Produce showed up in one of my dreams demonstrating how spirit guides sometimes play things out with us on the dream plane. Produce appeared in my dream as a thug. I intuitively knew this in the dream allowing me some sense of trust and the dream proceeded.

It was very dark outdoors as I stood on the sidewalk near the street. When I became aware in the dream, Produce was beating me with a piece of furniture and trying to force me into the car in front of us. I fought him but was physically too weak to overpower him and he had me sandwiched in between him and the car so I could not get away. He then took a wooden chair and continued to beat me until I got into the car. (I did not feel any physical pain in this dream, but I did feel terror.) At the time, I believed in *visualizing* the White Light whenever I felt a need for protection, but I was so frantic that I could not summon a visual image to save my life (pun intended). I sat in the back seat of the car trembling with fear for what seemed like an eternity. Finally, I suddenly began chanting, "White Light! White Light! White Light! " I looked into the rear view mirror from my place in the back seat and saw the White Light coming through the mirror towards me. That ended the dream; I knew I would be all right. I knew upon recalling the dream that is the mantra I am to use in an emergency, it is good to have one.

Merishkan and I lived in another house in Ohio City during the latter 1980's, I was leasing the house with option to buy. I was considering making the purchase and then renting it out. The neighborhood contained a mixture of diverse people, Hispanic, Black and White as well as varying levels of wealth. We were unaware when we took out the lease that there was a crack house around the corner. It was the oldest section of Cleveland and was undergoing a lot of renovation.

One evening Merishkan and I were conversing in the front room that had windows facing the street. The front door also faced the street and there was a chain-link fence around the house. Hearing some sort of a raucous, I went to the front door to see from where the noise was coming. There was a man on the other side of the street yelling at three teenage boys as though chastising them for something. He swore at them and called them names. The man stumbled and staggered, apparently drunk. He was very loud and disruptive. I became somewhat annoyed with his noise and spontaneously thought, "He's being disruptive, he should die." Merishkan came to the door to investigate too and I explained what I saw.

81

Subsequently we went back to our conversation in the living room.

In a few minutes, I grew curious and got up to see why it had become so quiet after such disruption. We both went to see what was happening. There was the man, lying face down and motionless in the street, where the alley intersects. We had not heard any gun shot and we could not see any signs of a wound or blood flowing from him. There was no trace of the three teen boys. Briefly we were wondering what to do when we saw an emergency vehicle, sans siren, drive up to the man lying in the street. They were near the alley that made a "T" at our street, so there was a street light above illuminating the scenario. After a long hesitation, the emergency medical technicians scooped him up and deposited him in the vehicle. They quietly drove off.

It took only a moment for me to remember my thought that this disruptive man should die. Immediately Merishkan dropped into trance. An angel named Alexander came through, knowing what I was thinking. He said that I did not harbor any malice at the time of my thought and that my manifestation angels, hearing my mental comment, arranged the script for the actors to play out. Knowing that we plan our deaths as well as our births and life lessons, I asked if this man's Karma was planned accordingly. Alexander answered in the affirmative. He came through to offer support and understanding that my thought did not kill this man. It was a combination of his wanting to leave the earth plane, of my thought and my manifestation angels taking action. But the experience did render me more deeply committed to watching my thoughts.

With regard to the crack house around the corner from where we were living, we also received interesting news about that. Since we were working with the angels and other unseen spiritual forces of Light, there was more spiritual energy around us wherever we lived. Just by living in this area, the Light Beings surrounding us brought balance and protection into our reality. The people living in the crack house were apprehended and removed; the house was subsequently torn down.

It was always interesting living with an Angelic "walk-in" channeler. Merishkan and I went to a Waldenbooks store and browsed for a couple of hours. Both of us being used to deep concentration, we left the store in altered state and walked out into the mall. As we meandered out of the entrance to the book store, I felt an impression on the right side of my head and "heard" that I should change my name to Michelle "Star" (not my birth name). At that very moment, we heard over the entire mall's public address system announcing in a sing-song sound, Michelle Sta-ar, Michelle Sta-ar

(Star, punctuation for emphasis). I was blown away! I told Merishkan that I was just thinking I should change my name to Michelle Star and he said that public announcement was my confirmation from Spirit. I learned later from the teller at my bank that there is another person with this name, but she spells it differently. I changed my name to Michelle Star legally in 1991.

Related to dreams and yet not dreaming, I experienced a whisper as I was coming back to the waking state on at least three occasions, several months apart. A guide, my Higher Self, someone was telling me that my father had sexually abused me as a baby. My response was not one of surprise, which *is* a surprise to me since I had never thought of it. I told the guide that I did not remember it but was open to exploring the issue. Nothing happened.

Another interesting phenomenon occurred that was not a dream, but an actual flashback. It was a most disturbing experience and I will explain first the background and then what happened.

In the late 1970's when I was still married, my husband had a partner with whom he jointly owned a private airplane. He and his partner shared the use of the plane and maintained a schedule so there was no conflict.

My then husband and I used to fly from the sod area at Cleveland Hopkins International airport for vacations and little hops to a nearby county airport for dinner. During one particular flight, we had taken off, traversed through a thick cover of clouds and lifted into a clear sky. I was still in my depressed state and looked over to my right and saw the gigantic, radiant sun. I innocently made the comment in realization, "Gee, the sun really does shine even when the sky is full of clouds." My husband was an intellectual and practical sort and thought I was cute and being "ditzy" making this comment. He practically let the plane drop out of the sky with laughter, totally missing the significance of such a statement. He was thinking, "Of course the sun shines above the clouds! " But at that time I was still in such a deep depression that I could not seem to grasp the fact that clouds merely cover the sun, not extinguish it, and that the sun did indeed prevail. Depression served as my own individual cloud blocking the sun's (Life's) nurturing rays. This incident was a metaphor for how I perceived Life then: I had for such a long time so little Light (sun) in my life (darkness) that I could not comprehend that clouds (challenges) merely overshadow the sun (Light/God/My Inner Light), and that the sun (Light/God/My Inner Light) actually did exist. I had just experienced an epiphany realizing that there was hope for me, Light existed above the abysmal darkness in which I was living—I only had to fly through the clouds to see the sun. My husband guffawed and howled as I continued my attempt to explain what I meant. I became very frustrated as he continued laughing at me, thinking I was ignorant of science and being "cute," not listening to me at all. If the plane had been bigger, he probably would have rolled in the aisle.

When Merishkan and I went to see my ex-husband in his office some 15 years later with a legal question, we listened as he felt compelled to tell his version of the story. He roared in laughter all over again nearly losing all control. I felt intensely frustrated because he still did not understand the deeper significance of what really happened. The frustration was so intense it catapulted me into altered state and I had a flashback to the day the original event happened in the plane--just for a second. In that moment, I was actually there, in living color. I instantly felt the depth of feelings I embodied at that time, sitting in the airplane peering over at the sun. I was shocked at the memory of how I lived in such darkness, anguish and depression. I had come such a long way from then and was so overcome by the re-experience of those feelings that I suddenly began to sob uncontrollably there in his office. And still he thought it was funny. I tried even through my tears to persuade him to listen to me. I wanted him to understand what really happened, but ultimately I failed.

Later, I talked with my guides in a channeling session. They told me that the only connection to Light I had growing up was my twin brother and our miniature Dachshund. My ex-husband's behavior and the flashback experience were part of a "cosmic set-up" meant to show me how far I had come in the span of fifteen or so years. Just like the plane rose above the clouds into open sky, I eventually rose above the depression and darkness I had experienced. My guides encouraged me to recognize all the healing I had done and to celebrate my achievement.

Next it was time for Merishkan and me to move back to the house where we lived before moving to the house in Ohio City.

# 14 Grand Initiation

Merishkan and I moved back to our earlier house, where Julie was still living. She was preparing to get married as she had found someone to share love and would soon be moving out. It was 1990 now and I was still estranged from my family. I missed them and at Christmas time snuck over to my parents' house and delivered presents for everyone because I couldn't bear to not give them gifts. It was late at night and they didn't know I had been there. I felt like a Santa Claus and imagined them finding their presents in the morning where I left them on the breezeway. I still stayed away. I needed more time to heal and release the rage and severe control issues I had accumulated.

Merishkan had started acting unusual. We laughed in good humor at his washing just the inside of the glasses. He said he was re-integrating but I did not question the significance of his statement. As "Coyote," Merishkan started to go out with a fellow to listen to a couple of bands at one or two bars. This fellow started coming to visit and even brought Coyote flowers on one occasion. I teased Merishkan about a fellow having a crush on him. Coyote started to cook according to this fellow's preferences, which meant hot dogs and baked beans. I was getting confused. When the Tarot Oracle channeled now, she called him the "Coyote-Merishkan blend." I ignored the signs trying to maintain *status quo*. I could feel Merishkan slipping away, out of my grasp. This was much too painful to acknowledge. One time he even said he was having trouble staying in the body as a walk-in and I offered to secure him through his chakras. This proved ineffective and I pushed the signs to the back of my mind. I felt as though he was avoiding me too.

It had been four years since Merishkan's arrival into my life (this time around). We had endured so much—doing, and undoing—over time. One evening when the three of us were hanging out at home, I was listening to the stereo. It was a one-piece floor model, long and narrow with a turntable inside and speakers on each end with sliding doors to cover them when not in use, and in Mediterranean motif with red velvet crisscrosses woven over the speakers. It sat in front of the picture window overlooking the front porch. Merishkan was working at the dining room table adjacent to the living room where I was and Julie was at the window seat in the dining room. All of us were within fairly close proximity.

The next song that I heard on the stereo was "Somewhere Out There" performed by Linda Ronstadt and James Ingram from the movie "American Tale." The music was incredibly beautiful and I lay on the floor with my head close to the speaker so I could hear it more clearly without distraction. Suddenly, I started to sob uncontrollably. I stood up and had another "intuitive flash." This one was so painful I could not speak. I received the transmission that Merishkan was going to leave me! Julie and Merishkan both were annoyed with me crying so hard over a song, but I could not speak of what I had just learned. I tried, but I just could not speak of it. These occasions bring so much frustration. The intensity was nearly intolerable—I could almost choke on it.

Produce channeled in right away and covered the event by telling us that I had "tuned in" to the musicians performing the song and had felt all of their emotions. In truth, I was not supposed to know that Merishkan was leaving; I pushed the information to the back of my mind because it was simply too painful to bear. I thought Merishkan was here for the duration of my life and it was shocking news. Produce' channel provided a temporary band aid of relief in comfortable denial.

A day or two later Merishkan and I were getting into the car and I again received the transmission that he was leaving. Again the pain was so intense and shocking that I could not address the issue. Soon, my Higher Self Spirit Guide Karl channeled through Coyote. He said that the deep spiritual love that existed between Merishkan and me had propelled our soul growth **ten**

**years** ahead of schedule. He said I had not intended to progress this far in this lifetime.

Within a few days, I was at home and looking for Merishkan. It was unusual that we were separated for very long and I wondered where he was. I noticed the door ajar to the bedroom Julie had used and she had moved out. I poked my head in and there was Merishkan (Coyote), lying on the bed. I asked what was going on and she said that she and this fellow had feelings for each other and they wanted to be together. I asked, "Where is Merishkan?" She responded, "He is here." I demanded, "Where?" She shrugged her shoulders and looked away. Again, shock. I asked where he had gone and she could not answer me.

I became enraged. All the rage and resentment of my lifetime surfaced and blew out through my chakras, clearing everything. One of the angels that channeled, Alexander, was a specialist in anger. He used to try to make me angry when he was in channel and I never complied. Now it ALL came forth in a wave of heat and anger and I shouted at her, "I hate you, I HATE you! Get out of this house!" Soon her fellow came to get her and she ended up moving in with him. Within a month they were married.

I had never felt that degree of anger ever in my life. I was still seething with venomous anger and I had no control over the situation. Now, I take that back. I felt close to this level of anger at my mother—when I was a young teen and ended up beating myself in the stomach or throwing a pillow across my bedroom. I hated my mother to the point that at one time that I wanted to murder her. I would not ever act on that thought, but I could understand people that did commit murder, for lesser reasons. All of this was up for review and resolution. Pent-up anger has to come out somehow.

There is no description for the devastation I felt. I went down to the Yoga room in the basement and tried to meditate. When I closed my eyes, I immediately had another vision. This time it was a patch of colorful Forget-Me-Not flowers that suddenly *burst* onto the screen of my inner vision. I knew the flowers were from Merishkan or Karl, and needing some semblance of support, I asked to see them once more. Again they burst onto the screen of my inner vision. Someone cared enough to send them even a second time, someone was listening.

Now I was alone. I remember while he was still here asking Merishkan about all the channeling and the answers that were brought through. I said, "Merishkan, I know that I am supposed to be able to get my answers from inside myself, and yet you have been bringing me answers through channeling and your wisdom. What's going to happen?" He responded in a gentle tone, "You didn't believe you could access and trust your answers from within, so they (the angels and Kali) sent me." He continued nonchalantly, "They will turn you back into yourself."

Here it was. I was being turned back into myself. Ow.

# 15 THE AFTERMATH

It is June, 1990. I was totally alone. Merishkan was gone—disappeared without a good-bye, unless the Forget-Me-Nots count. Coyote was gone. My beloved guide Karl was gone—I had to go through a guide change. (This happens when you and your guide have reached the pinnacle of working together.) I could feel no one spirit side. The friends Merishkan and I had were gone--they didn't understand what happened, I barely understood it myself. One friend felt slighted because she was not privy to the fact that Merishkan was a walk-in. She left in disgust. I felt as though I had fallen into a black hole where no one could find me. Grief-stricken, it seemed like time had ceased to exist. Having cleansed my chakra line through an eruption the human counterpart of Mount St. Helens, I had to live through the "dark night of the soul" referenced in so many metaphysical writings. Joseph Campbell writes in *The Hero with a Thousand Faces* that this type of experience is a descent "into the womb of the Goddess" or like Jonah, down into the "belly of the whale." He eloquently describes the plot of "wrenching the love object away" and the subsequent journey through the trials of the initiation. My symptoms exactly!

Things were so dark I had to go deep within to search for the Light. My energy centers were purged and cleansed from all previous blockages. In this experience, I felt the stored anger of all forty-four years of my lifetime at once. Here was the calm after the explosion. The meadows and green fields of love and life were dead and covered in ash to become fertile again. I knew at some level I had agreed to this event, but I could hardly believe it. Things were so dark I arduously searched for the Light at the foundation of my essence. What better place to find it. "Finding the Light" represents accessing the benign power within call it God, Goddess, Higher Self or all of the above, and forging a bonded relationship with it.

This experience was an initiation, a rite of passage, offered by the Goddess Kali. I am now her initiate, meaning I serve her and align with her objectives (i.e., bringing balance and creativity, the Feminine Principle, back to the planet). I learned from another source that the walk-ins on the Earth at that time working in cooperation with Kali were here for the purpose of staging this initiation. They were to prepare the Masters, those at a certain level of evolution and participating in this "play," to blaze trails in overcoming old programming and useless patriarchal scripts in order to help others that choose the path of enlightenment and oneness. The ascension is a choice to transcend the old paradigms and step into a new world of higher vibration in addition to bringing back the Feminine Principle that has been banned from the planet for so long. This will bring balance and Unity. I was to heal myself now, the rest of the way—alone. Intuition is the strongest quality in my astrology chart—it was time to develop and use it for the higher good.

In the days after Coyote and Merishkan's departure, chaos came in their place. I was working for two attorneys in a small law office in downtown Cleveland. I took the job because I thought a smaller office would have less stress. One attorney was an alcoholic bordering on retirement and the other one was bordering on bankruptcy. His passion was cooking gourmet meals instead of cooking up strategies for his clients, so he spent much of his time in his friend's nearby restaurant, living his dream and ignoring his law practice. Meanwhile, my checks were starting to bounce and the electric company had come to turn off the electricity. The first time, I paid the bill so I could still use the computer, but since it took forever to get reimbursed by the attorneys, the next time the electric company representative came, I just gave a message to the attorney. I needed to find a new job.

I arranged an interview at one of the larger law firms in downtown Cleveland. I was already reeling from the Merishkan events, but now I was facing a panel of three interviewers from the firm's human resource department. I had to tell them why I wanted to work at their firm and in what department. I didn't know what department so I told them off the top of my head the workers' compensation area. It was the right answer; it turned out they needed someone in that department. They required me to return for two more interviews, but I did get the job.

As an addition to the chaos, I became overwhelmed and lost my keys— to the house, the car and the van, which had no duplicate so I had to have the locksmith come out and make one.

While Merishkan was here, he bought a half-wolf/half-Shepherd hybrid dog, a male puppy. I had adopted a six-month old Malamute male puppy from the Animal Protective League and he loved to tease the puppy. You can believe it when you hear that wolves have memory. This dog soon proved it. We took in a third dog that showed up in our back yard that was the reincarnation of the puppy I loved as a little girl. (Yes, dogs reincarnate.) She was very Doxie-like but was quite round. Merishkan called her Sausage-Kielbasa and the name stuck. So I was left with three dogs. The half-wolf's memory kicked in at this point, remembering the haughty tormenting from my Malamute as the two dogs reached adulthood. They started fighting. I had to somehow separate them. These were stand-up-on-the-hind-legs-and-bite-to-draw-blood fights. As painful as it was, I returned my injured and bleeding Malamute to the APL just for his own protection. I thought Coyote was going to take her dog but it turned out she couldn't have him where she lived, so I was stuck with the half-wolf and Sausage-Kielbasa. The half-wolf hybrid dog was busy during the day while I was gone at work. Sausage-Kielbasa had just gone into her first heat and he was forceful in trying to mate with her. There was blood everywhere, all over the house. By this time, I was at a total loss. I gave up and took both dogs to the APL and released them. It was extremely painful as I loved all three beautiful dogs and I know they were afraid, but I just couldn't handle any more drama, I already had so much on my plate. I drew the line. Now that Merishkan was gone, I was left to clean up the mess.

There is a movie with a line that I have remembered since this experience: "Tears melt the heart frozen in grief." That is it, in a nutshell. My grief melted my hard heart closed through fear and childhood losses.

Over the next five years, I continued the grief process over the loss of my creative child that left at the onset of attending the Baptist Church, the loss of my power of choice and ability to act--the loss of all personal power and intuition. Being buried by trauma after trauma was darkness enough no matter in what life it happened. I was concerned at times as to whether I would find my way back to the Light. Would I fail this initiation? As I mentioned previously, my twin brother and my miniature Doxie were my only connections to Light. But this was a surrender of me to my Higher Self or God/dess—a necessary step on the path of mysticism—releasing ego. The universal rug was pulled out from under me demonstrating the Divine Paradox in action: to release control is precisely how to gain it. I had to be willing to go through this experience, survive it, recognize, rebuild and reconnect with my creative aspect and my autonomy. It afforded me the ultimate opportunity to *transcend.* The plan worked, but I would not want to go through that again!

Once the proverbial dust settled and chaos subsided for the most part, I returned to my meditation practice. I was amazed at this first meditation experience.

I found myself transported to the center of the Earth with a group of other women. We formed a circle around the Earth's magma center at her core, and holding hands, danced in joy and glee. This told me I was not alone in this initiation. At first I could not understand how I could be in such a state of anguish over my recent losses in the physical plane and in such a state of joy in the spiritual. Then I realized we are multi-dimensional creatures and the pain or suffering we experience in this one is but the "twinkling of an eye" in the Universal scheme of things. I later realized I could change my focus to experience a positive creation in life by staying in the present moment. I learned that there truly is *only* the Eternal Now, in alignment with Eckhart Tolle's presentation in his book, *The Power of Now*.

As I returned to a more natural routine balancing work, Yoga and meditation, I became peaceful and healing continued. I bargained with Ashero that if he would help me sell the house, I would use part of the money to go to Kripalu. I invited my realtor to come to the house and start the paperwork on the New Moon in December, 1994. Within two weeks, on December 22, my father's birthday, the house sold and the purchaser paid cash for it! In June of 1995, after studying Yoga for 15 years and teaching Yoga for 10 years, I drove to Kripalu Yoga and Health Center in Massachusetts for teacher training and certification. With my ego still flagging, I thought I knew a lot and would be able to demonstrate my wisdom at Kripalu. The great thing about going to a school for 30 days, away from the distractions of the world and being totally immersed in the Yoga lifestyle is you can really hear and see your egoic behavior. I embarrassed myself when I attempted a body roll on the floor to show someone how it was done and landed on my face. I was eager but still had ego to contend with. A work in progress… Kripalu was perfect for me, the guru had left so I didn't have to submit to someone else's dogma which was part of the reason I chose this school. I remember being in class with 44 of my classmates, engaged in a spinal twist that caused my head to turn toward the opened door at the right front of the sanctuary. There was a bush clothed in flowers within view and a hummingbird darted in and out of the blossoms. There was also a Robin's nest in a bush outside the dormitory window and we got to watch the eggs hatch and the mother feed her babies. Synchronously, the day we graduated from the training, the babies left their nest too.

I also worked with John Bradshaw's work, *Homecoming* as well as his other books and Merishkan and I watched his lectures on PBS during the time we lived in Ohio City. This material was extremely helpful. Bradshaw gave exercises to help participants retrieve some of their lost memories and creativity. One experience was particularly heartwarming for me. Bradshaw recommended going into meditation stepping backwards in time to talk with the three-year-old self. We were to ask the child to go get whatever it wanted to bring along as it was coming home with the adult self. I sat in a wicker rocker for the exercise and I could see little Michelle as she went to retrieve her treasures. She came back with our Doxie dog and my twin brother! I explained to her that Buddy could come with us for a while, but eventually he would probably need to go with Big Bud. How adorable little children are—and to think for many years I didn't like them. The healing continued as I worked unremittingly. All I ever wanted was peace and I knew this was one way to uncover it.

My memories of life during the holocaust started emerging shortly after the dust settled on the explosive event with Coyote and friend. I spontaneously remembered that Julie was in that life with me. Then I remembered she was a man... she was my romantic partner and was enlisted in Hitler's army. I remembered being very thin physically and that I was not Jewish. I remembered the feelings of weakness and anguish. And, I remembered Julie as this man picking me up and carrying me toward a mass grave. He was preparing to throw me in with the others who were already dead. I pleaded with him, feebly whispering with tears in my throat, "Please don't do this, I'm not dead yet." I can still see the expression on his face, tight-lipped and stern with what appeared to be anguish behind his eyes, as he walked to the huge expanse of a grave. He showed no shred of mercy. He could not. He would have been shot to death. He threw me into the grave to be buried alive.

The start of this memory began when the three of us lived together, Julie, Merishkan and me. Part of what brought this to light was when I was resting and Merishkan came into my room describing a phone conversation he had just finished with the primary occupant's younger sister. She mentioned that she had found kittens that had been buried alive. I went into a panic for what seemed like an hour. I was very upset with her for telling me about the kittens. However, the underlying issue and reaction stemmed from my ability to relate all too well with the sensation of being buried alive. I could still feel the suffocation. My childhood, with two Earth sign parents, also felt like being buried alive.

I began to hate Julie for "killing" me, and there we were living in the same house. That can be a problem with other-life recall. We don't always get complete understanding right away—especially when the information comes in pieces. But the Universe (Higher Self and Guides) arranges "cosmic set-ups" and scenarios to assist with the healing process. My guide warned me that I was reducing my spiritual bank by the hatred I felt. I took his advice to heart and started changing my attitude.

Now living alone and getting back to the business of more clearing, I experienced over the next few weeks instances of turning on the television to see documentaries about the Holocaust showing emaciated people, wearing only the clothing of humiliation, being prepared for their trek to the gas chambers. One time, I was going to work at the office in downtown Cleveland, and having just disembarked from the rapid transit train heard peoples' footsteps on the terrazzo floor that immediately catapulted me to when I could hear Hitler's army on the march. Another experience was of being in both incarnations at once, similar to the Witch life as I was being escorted to my death. Once, I had decided to use the self-cleaning feature on my oven. It was the first time using that feature on this fairly new, high quality stove. The sickening stench from the oven prompted my memory of being alive around burning flesh in the camp during the Holocaust. After the odor was fully distributed through the house, I happened to turn on the television. Maybe you guessed it—another documentary on the Holocaust showing depressing film footage of those dear people preparing for Death's release.

How would you make peace with such hell on earth? Over time, I began to feel compassion for Julie in this life and as my mate in that life. If he had not followed orders when he took me to the mass grave, he would probably have been killed too. I began to understand his position, resigning myself to the tiny consolation that if it had to be someone carrying me off to my live burial ground, I would rather he perform the evil deed than some stranger. My compassion stretched and I made peace with the situation knowing there was a much higher purpose in the events of that time. In due course, acceptance of the events as I understood them, compassion and forgiveness delivered my healing and opened my heart.

I began studying alternative healing modalities when my friend Jean, a Yoga teacher and Phoenix Rising Yoga Therapist, called me one day to offer a new program that she had designed herself. She had a Master's degree and taught in schools so was well educated and organized. I enthusiastically agreed to take the course. There were fifteen of us all together and it took most of the summer to learn and practice in order to pass the certification exam. It was great fun practicing on each other, lying on a massage or Reiki table and giving each other this modality. I even went into altered state and remembered working as a healer on Atlantis. There, we worked in teams in a dimly lit structure that was shaped like a pyramid, but joined at the floor was another pyramid, pointing down into the Earth.

With all the issues I had growing up I must have somehow stockpiled my sense of humor. When one of the other students was working on me with the technique we learned, she merely mentioned she could see pink balloons around me. For some reason, that imagery was a trigger and I started laughing hysterically, and loudly, which was highly unusual for me. I never laughed that long, hard or loud ever before or since. Perhaps I tapped into a pocket of joy just waiting for the right moment to be released. It did seem easier to laugh after that!

Knowing Jean was great, she was a delightful person, very intelligent and we shared our passion for Yoga. I remember planning a lunch date with her to meet at the restaurant near the Wellness Center where she conducted her classes and workshops. The night before our lunch date, I had a dream with Jean and another healer friend from the East side of Cleveland. I had just come back from seeing my father after I confronted him about the sexual abuse to which my guides hinted as I awoke some mornings. He denied any wrongdoing – *and billed me for his time!* I wailed vehemently three times and felt intense energy exit through my solar plexus each time, similar to when I processed the Witch life, but this time it exited out the front of my body. Jean and my other friend tried to console me and were very supportive.

At lunch with Jean the next day, I described the dream to her. She said we could go over to the Wellness Center and go into meditation to see what we could learn. Are you sensing another "cosmic set-up?" You are so right!

After we ate, we left the restaurant and walked over to the nearby Center. We sat cross-legged on the floor and went into a meditative state. We started to converse about what was happening. Almost immediately, I felt heat around the left side of my face and ear. It became so hot that I mentioned it to Jean. She came closer and could see that my face and left ear were indeed inflamed and red. This elicited visuals on the screen of my mind. My body remembered, holding the memory in my cells all these years, then providing intense sensation so I could tap into the memory.

I saw a dark room. I could not tell if the room was intentionally darkened or if my meditation was dark. It for certain was not in color as some of my dreams and visions have been. I was sitting across from a closed door, the entrance into the room. It was very difficult to see where I was, but it looked like a garage or machine shop. I saw my father enter through the door. He was young like in some of the pictures of him I've

95

seen long since then. I felt prompted to look down at myself and saw that I was naked and appeared to be about a year old. I again looked at my father and noticed I could see his aura, his energy field, which was filled with tiny bugs all around him. I didn't know what that meant, I just could see them. He walked over toward me. He held me in a strange way, holding onto my head—I tried to push him away and said, "Daddy, stop, that hurts." Even though he was hurting me, I felt love for him. I just wasn't strong enough to push him away. He said nothing but I then felt warm moisture in and around my ear. Jean said, "Your skin was very soft." He used my one-year old face for his pleasure. I thought she was going to comfort me around this, but she simply announced, "You're going to have to heal that," and walked away. My jaw dropped. I was now age 50, it was 1996. I had been working on healing myself and working through other lifestreams which ultimately built a strong enough container for me to handle this memory. My prayers for healing blockages, upon the recognition I did not have a happy romantic relationship and had trouble manifesting sufficient income, had been answered. The whispers from guides planting the seed of knowledge were now permanently hushed. But my friend was right. I needed to heal this issue.

Not too long after that lunch date and the healing course finished, I signed up for the three levels of Reiki healing. Interesting, I realized that the other friend in my dream with Jean hosted the Reiki Master from Sedona that taught the course in her office on the east side. Once I finished Reiki training, I started offering appointments, and of course I magnetized other women that had been sexually abused. Between Yoga and Reiki and Jean's technique, I personally was healing more (healing always goes both ways) and I had a few more memories of my father using my body. There was never any penetration, but I felt my innocence was taken from me regardless. As Buz Myers stated in my astrology consultation with him, "My father killed my self-esteem." Perhaps now it is easier to understand why I would want to commit suicide. But Buz also told me that I could not get out of this life until I achieved my purpose. That is partly why I didn't die when I made the attempt. In setting up this life, we (my guides and I) blocked any escape until my purpose was accomplished. But Buz didn't tell me what my purpose is! I would have to do more searching.

It was through another astrologer that I learned that I am "Guruampura," meaning I come through an uninterrupted line of gurus. As we talked during the consultation, we determined that my father was the one that brought me in through this line. I suspect that is also where Ashero fits in. This was the connection, the spiritual bond I had with my father that made my mother so jealous. And I believe this bond is what made it easier to forgive my father for his drunken actions, in addition to the fact I was so young, I didn't understand it was aberrant behavior. I knew we had established an agreement before incarnating to do this, even intuitively as a child. I was clearing karma from a time when I myself abused children. The energy is now balanced. All is well.

I learned later that bugs in the aura are indicative of alcoholism. Others with the gift of "second sight" or clairvoyance have seen them too.

# 16 WORK AND FAMILY –OR– FAMILY AND WORK

Having obtained my Yoga teacher's certification in June 1995, I was driven to obtain more education. In August, I enrolled in the YogaRhythmics/DansKinetics course in Sumneytown, Pennsylvania which was the location of the original Kripalu. This course was about dancing through the chakras and was an intensive course that provided much needed healing for everyone in the class. I had trouble paying for the course right on the heels of my Kripalu training, but it seemed an important course to take. I was allowed to catch up by making payments in smaller increments. When I returned home, I continued to teach Yoga, DansKinetics and offered Tarot readings. We had six months to complete assignments after getting home that ensured we were practicing DK and experiencing our feelings. We were required to practice DK and journal on a daily basis in order to complete the certification which was a great discipline.

A few weeks before, during the course and after I returned, I was experiencing severe lower back pain. With such weakness from childhood, now as an aspiring Yogini (female Yoga practitioner) and DK dancer, my back was speaking loudly to me. I was accustomed to making visits to the chiropractor from the start of my dance and exercise programs. Having phased out my jogging program years before, I needed to see what might be causing the back pain. I returned to the chiropractor. When the assistant measured my height, she said I was 5'5" and I said, "Oh no, that's not right, I'm 5'5½"! " She insisted I was 5'5," showed me the measurement scale, and in I went for x-rays. When they were ready, the chiropractor showed me where my spinal column was degenerating. He said the debris from the disks degenerating at L5-S1 area was causing the pain. And, I was shocked to learn I had lost a half inch off my height! There was about half my disk remaining and he said it *could* grow back. I was determined to do just that.

# I Forgive You, Daddy – Yoga and the Angels Healed Me!

I put myself on a program of more introspection to release stored emotion and increased Yoga/meditation, integrating more arches and back bending. My back was so painful I would lie in bed on a tennis ball providing pressure to release tight muscles. Later I used a knobble, a wooden massage device to apply the pressure. Every time I did this work, I would get very sleepy from the toxins and debris released and would usually have to sleep. I also realized that I was practicing from ego when I performed forward bends (Paschimottanasana in Sanskrit, seated head-to-knee pose in English) and just wanted to show off stretching my torso down to my legs as though folding in half. The problem was I avoided the backward bending poses that would have balanced my practice. Small wonder, my lower back is where much of my fear was stored. I did not want to face it. Also, as Merishkan mentioned in the Tarot reading in Chapter X, I had grown up spineless and had not developed sufficient personal power to create a strong spine and musculature.

I continued working with arching and back bending Yoga poses like Camel, Pigeon and Wheel and took 1,000 mg. of Glucosamine for several years. The Glucosamine helped reduce inflammation and re-build the cartilage in my disks. It took concerted effort on a daily basis to achieve healing, along with recognizing emotions that surfaced during my work. It was a gradual improvement, so gradual that I'm not sure when it happened, but checking in after 10 years and re-measuring my height, I had re-grown that half inch!   The chiropractor said that if there was any disk left in a degenerative condition, it could conceivably be re-grown and brought back to health. My understanding is this is an uncommon occurrence. It was well worth the effort though and I learned to do backbends again in the process. During my training at the dance studio from age 23 through 34, I was at times involved with gymnastics where my back hurt a great deal in working on backbends. My spine needed a slower opening to honor the emotional body. It was important to keep up though, bending backwards is grounding. With no practical, grounding Earth element in my natal chart, I needed grounding!

After Merishkan and Coyote left, I eventually reconnected with my family. I was depressed and they blamed Merishkan, but provided support for me. As I continued on my healing journey, my sister and brother came to visit. They were still filled with childhood anger and resentment so it was difficult to relate with them. I was still working through my own stored emotions. I tried to explain to them that Merishkan was an angel that had "traded places" with the soul of Coyote, but it was too far beyond their capacity to accept. I cried when I told them that his leaving was an initiation for me, but they couldn't grasp this reality. I had to let it go and just accept whatever relationship I could nurture with them.

At Thanksgiving, dinner was being served at my sister's house. I remember having a "psychic moment" with her as we stood at the kitchen sink. I was being more my "happy-go-lucky" self, talking with her about how it's good to wash the pots and pans before eating dinner so we didn't have that to contend with along with all the serving dishes after. She was quiet and looked over at me. I glimpsed down at her heart chakra over the sternum. I saw streams of energy leaving her heart chakra and curving around towards me. I felt love from her and was just about to say "I love you," when my guide said, "Wait! " He conveyed to me that she was not ready to hear those words verbally so I sent her the message through telepathy. Our family never learned to say the words to each other, so I held back until a later time when we were more open. When I went to the anger management support group those few times, the facilitator told me I needed 12 hugs a day, 6 a day just for maintenance. I told a couple friends at work and we started hugging. I told my parents and we started hugging too, but "I love you" was a bit much for my big sister at that time. Later, they would become very important words...

At Christmas that year, my parents and sister came over to my house and helped me decorate the tree. During the Holidays I was depressed at the losses I'd gone through, so it was nice to be around family. I had bought one last live tree remembering how Merishkan had taught Julie and me how to tune in to the tree spirit. Some of them love to be all dressed up and honored during our celebrations. One even stayed, transferring its consciousness for a while into a horse head skull Merishkan displayed arranged in an art piece. We could feel its icy-cold life force move slowly into the skull. We had great affection for it. I stopped buying live trees though--it broke my heart to sever a tree's connection to the Earth. I can appreciate and enjoy them right where they are, rooted in the ground. I met them in my dreams anyway, so didn't need to cut any down.

In 1999, I returned to Kripalu to study Integrative Yoga Therapy with Joseph LePage. It was a two-week course with high intensity and long days, but it clarified more spiritual workings and the holistic approach using Yoga as a therapeutic tool. Some of the students had difficulty tolerating the intensity and would "space out," starting to giggle or laugh. It was a little disruptive, especially from adults, but I totally understood. Joseph created a scholarly manual for our course that was creatively written and informative. We were required to read all 1500 pages before we could receive our certificates and I wanted to finish as soon as I could. I had been hired by the Cleveland Clinic to teach the classes for an upcoming study being conducted by Sonia Gaur, M.D., then a psychiatric resident and wanted to have my certification in tact at the outset. The Clinic's scientific study started in March, 2000 entitled, "The Impact of Yoga on a Chronic Pain Population," and allowed me to demonstrate how Yoga can be used as a therapeutic tool for a range of physical and emotional challenges. The conclusion of the study revealed that "Yoga improves mood in chronic pain patients, leads to decreased medication use, and a decrease in pain severity. Results are statistically significant." I thought I was going to be able to teach classes at the conclusion of the study, but that didn't happen until years later. I did get permission to order a copy of the 4' x 6' vinyl poster displayed at the residents' reception – it cost me $200, but I felt I could use it at health fairs to establish greater validity for Yoga—and me.

It was a challenge to give these Clinic classes since I was working full-time plus overtime in the law office, gave three weekly Yoga classes of my own and three classes per week for the Clinic study. On top of all that, I was trying to work with a vegetarian meal plan. I just didn't have the time to do it justice and didn't feel very well on that diet. I stayed with it for a while longer. At least the past-life recall and family issues had subsided so I could work on building confidence and creating some success in my life.

I was delighted a year later in 2001 while still working downtown in the law firm to be invited to offer a workshop at both days of the National Respiratory Care and Critical Care Nurses' Conference also held downtown. It was exciting because I was in the company of scientists and I received the same level of pay. There were about 250 people in my workshops and they seemed receptive to my talk, "Yoga for Health – Yours & Others." I interspersed some energy exercises and Yoga poses that were fun and added interest to the lecture. I felt honored to be included and thought maybe success was finally coming to meet me.

My last legal assistant position before leaving the field to teach Yoga full-time was working for a 28-year-old, short, overweight bully from Michigan. He was extremely bright with a quick mind and a lively sense of humor. I actually liked this guy a lot; he had a great "kid" quality about him at times. I watched him interact with others and witnessed his tongue-in-cheek humor, but he was hired to use his tyrannical tactics on the opposition. He talked so fast that to me it sounded like he was speaking a foreign language. My desk was just outside his office where I could hear every profane word he uttered. He was loud and vulgar even though he had a brilliant mind for legal work he never took a break from profanity. He typed on the computer as swiftly as he spoke. He became impatient with me when I did not understand the demands he spit out to perform some task or if I made a mistake. I became so nervous that I made more mistakes—some even surprised me, they were so blatant.

Once, one of the senior partners that occupied the office next door came to his office, sat down and told him he found his language highly offensive and unacceptable and he wanted it to stop. The partner spoke on my behalf as well peering out at me where I sat behind my desk, knowing I was exposed to this language too. The bully refused to make any adjustment in his speech or attitude as requested and he merely closed his door to muffle his language for a few days, eventually fully maintaining his previous behavior—with the door open.

I could not get this fellow to discuss what he wanted or how I could improve—he always blew me off. Nor could I spend enough hours practicing Yoga to overcome the stress I was feeling; I became somewhat depressed feeling my hands were tied.   Finally, one day this young fellow accused me of a mistake that I knew I did not make. I had worked with him longer than any other assistant in that law firm—a year and a half—and I reached saturation. I stood at my desk and surrendered the stress. I did not care if I lost my job I was not going to tolerate this situation any longer. *I felt an immense release of energy that drained out of my entire body and exited through my feet.* With this release came the knowing in that moment I would not accept this treatment any longer. Feeling no fear whatsoever, I confidently walked over to the doorway of his office and announced that I could not work with him anymore. He replied, "I'm not going to argue with you about this." I told him, "I'm not arguing with you about it, I can't do this anymore. I simply will not work with you! " I felt strong, empowered and decisive. He just sat, short as he was, peering over his desk appearing small. He silently rolled his eyes and went back to what he was doing. I immediately called my coordinator to report the sequence of events—unfortunately she was out for the entire day. I left her a long voice mail message explaining exactly what happened. The next day she came up to my desk and was angry about the situation--until I explained further. The message I left didn't sufficiently get the point across. But, once she understood the situation, she immediately moved me to another desk away from the bully.

The coordinator assigned another assistant to work with this attorney. Days later, as I walked by the desk where she had replaced me, I began to chat lightly with the new assistant about what happened. She adamantly claimed she would never let anyone talk to her that way. In the back of my mind, I wondered how she would stop him, but then perhaps she had higher self-esteem than I and could deal with him more effectively. It only took a couple of weeks to learn that this guy talked to the new assistant "that way," *and* he was so impactful about it she was driven to tears. She not only left the position working for this attorney, she left the firm completely after years of service. She took a job across the street with a competitor.

A short time later, the secretarial coordinator called me into her office. She apologized to me about the bully situation and told me that the partners of the firm held a meeting where they unanimously decided *never* to hire someone with the aggressive "bully" personality type again. He was assigned to work with one of the senior partners as his mentor and was watched very closely from that point on.

In about three months, December 2002, I turned in my notice at the law firm to follow my dream to teach Yoga full-time. My heart was being drawn to my beloved Mohican State Park outside of Loudonville, OH. With my history of being disconnected from my intuition, I decided to get a reading from a well-respected Spiritualist Minister woman near Akron to help me determine if moving was in my best interest. I had bought another house and would have to rent it out, but I felt a longing to move to beautiful Loudonville. Eileen was gifted psychically and welcomed me into her starlit, faery infused reading room. She told me that I am an angel and that meant my mother was too (apparently angels beget angels). She said the Angels missed me and I should reconnect with them in meditation. She went through my childhood and early adult life events with great accuracy, much to her chagrin. She didn't want to go to the time around my attempt. She said it was too dark. Her guides pressed her to go on. She said one of my directions this life is to find my inner father, the protector. She also said my soul needed to live in Loudonville at this time and she recommended moving there. This is just what I wanted to hear.

I put an ad in the Loudonville paper inquiring as to how many people would be interested in having Yoga classes there. I got about 30 affirmative responses and felt that was sufficient to warrant a move. I secured a renter for the house, packed my belongings and headed south to beauty's embrace.

Nothing is ever the way we think it will be, but I had not learned that yet. I had a wonderful apartment on the third floor above a restaurant with beams across the ceilings that my two cats could access and thoroughly enjoyed for chasing wildebeests. There was a spiral wrought-iron railing leading up to a cozy loft where I placed my bedroom. I put rope lighting around the railing that cast a dreamy glow out into the living room/Yoga room. There was enough open space for 10 students to take class. I started classes right away so I could begin building income. People started coming but they were sporadic in their attendance. It was a different mentality there. Some lived on farms where they had to attend to cows and were sometimes late to class. They were lovely people though.

After I got settled in, I started driving to Mohican to meditate. There was hardly anyone there in the early mornings so I had the place to myself. I relaxed and enjoyed the woods, the Gorge, all things nature. I made friends with students and a couple of them would play with Tarot. I even taught them Tarot for a while. My soul was inspired and I was approaching happiness. Money was becoming scarce though so I took a part-time job doing some home health care. The one couple I provided services for lived in the country where I had to drive up a long hill to get to their house. When it snowed, my car wouldn't make it, so sometimes I had to wait until the road was treated so I could get to my destination. Things were so different here. My sister came down to visit me and we watched in awe as the workmen dismantled the Ferris wheel from the annual street fair in front of my living room window.

In 2004, I was offered work teaching Yoga for two women physical therapist partners that formed a small company that provided continuing education seminars. A fellow had been giving the class but he wanted out so he could spend more time with his son. I stepped into the job which involved traveling to Detroit, Pittsburgh, Fort Wayne, Columbus, Cleveland and Dayton to give 6-hour seminars on Yoga for OT/PTs and other body workers to take back to their clinics. It paid very well; when I had to travel out of state, I was paid double. Traveling two or three times in a month was challenging as my body is used to a lot of movement. Sitting in the car for hours driving to/from my destinations was difficult. I loved it, though it could sometimes be lonely during those long drives. But I was doing what I loved. Then, in 2005, I learned my mother was having health challenges and I felt a need to move back to my hometown where she and my father lived. I got help from a friend that had a pickup truck and the two of us moved all my possessions to an apartment on the outskirts of my hometown. My parents were aging with accompanying health concerns and my sister being the oldest of the children did a lot of work for them. She also was the most family oriented having three sons and worked hard to keep the whole family together. She saw to it that my parent's funeral arrangements, wills and living wills were all in place and everything was in order. It was like pulling teeth for her to get them to take action, but she was a strong and persistent person, so she got things done, parents being irritable all the way.

## I Forgive You, Daddy – Yoga and the Angels Healed Me!

I continued teaching and traveling after I moved but was now conveniently closer to my parents. Time flew by and 2008 was upon me. My parents were still living at home when my mother started having hallucinations. We siblings learned that Dad knew of this for about a year without revealing the truth to anyone. We were all concerned for her; all three of us started keeping a closer watch on both of them. Dad was already having TIA's (transient ischemic attacks or "mini strokes") and shouldn't be driving, but being the stubborn German he was, he refused to relinquish his keys. He was prone to falling even in his younger days and had several falls at home, so we became more vigilant. And Mom was pointing to a little girl outdoors and across the street—that little girl wasn't really there, not in my reality anyway.

Now that I was within a five-minute drive to my sister's, I saw her more often. She was having a lot of back pain and had just recovered for the most part from a severe bronchial condition. I was giving her Reiki treatments for her back and could tell there were places where there was no vital life force. I mentioned to her that I felt there was something seriously wrong. She still had a cough from the bronchitis that she couldn't get rid of and scheduled an appointment for the doctor to check her. Then she gave us the news. My sister was diagnosed with Stage 4 non-Hodgkin's Lymphoma. The doctor said it was old and had been there a long time. My intuition kicked in and I felt a bleak outlook. She was only 65.

I did my best to try to convince my sister to explore alternative methods before she went the traditional chemo and radiation route. I knew personally of others that had recovered completely from the same diagnosis using other more natural methods. But she ultimately chose the doctor's recommendations. The next time I visited my sister, she announced her decision to take chemo and radiation and her middle son Jeff would be the one to drive her to her appointments. But intuitively I knew when she told me of her decision that she was going to die. I could barely hold back the sobs.

With my sister incapacitated and my twin brother being a Viet Nam Veteran with many of his own health problems, I was the one left to help our parents. Everyone was doing the best they could at the time, including me.

My next visit to see my parents, I walked into the living room and heard my mother screaming in pain. She was lying on the floor with Dad standing over her. She didn't want us to call 9-1-1 because she thought the pain would subside, but she couldn't even move. I made the call and she was taken to the emergency room. Mom had broken her femur near her hip and required surgery. She slipped on a stack of magazines that were piled near her favorite living room chair and couldn't keep from falling. I could barely endure seeing her in so much pain. But after surgery and a little time to recuperate, she was released from the hospital and taken to the nursing home for rehab. My sister had dropped out of sight with reactions to the cancer treatments.

The job I had traveling and teaching Yoga came to an end in 2008, the same year my sister was diagnosed and my mother fell. People were now looking to the internet for their continuing education and the OT ladies were going out of their continuing education business. They worked traditional jobs so were in no danger financially, but it was sad to see the gig end for all of us. Now I was struggling to find sufficient teaching jobs to pay the bills. I did secure some very nice opportunities, but it wasn't enough to sustain living expenses. I was going to have to move back to the City. I moved in with my dear friend John who was kind and generous and allowed me to bring my two kitties. Shortly after moving, I did manage to secure a teaching position with the Cleveland Clinic. I was now an employee and taught several evenings a week. I was so happy to be teaching Yoga there and wanted to share that with my sister, but she needed privacy. The Yoga students were wonderful and appreciated receiving Yoga.

My sister continued to be injected with what she called "poison" and I was still at a loss around her decision. I would try to visit her, but her husband usually said, "She's sleeping now." I knew she and Mom would miss each other so I bought cards from each one to the other and bought little trinkets so they would have remembrances that each was loved by the other. I would take one card to my sister to try and sign to give to our Mom, and then take another card to my Mom for her to sign for my sister. It worked for a while, but sometimes I had to leave my sister's present on the doorstep. She just couldn't accept company.

My mother was very unhappy in the nursing home. She was confused and angry and after a couple weeks started to refuse occupational and physical therapy. She even hit one of the therapists during a tantrum. There was a history in that place that she didn't want to remember. Her mother was placed in that nursing home with arteriosclerosis and eventually died there, her oldest sister was placed there for her last years suffering with severe osteoporosis and she eventually died there. She helped take care of both of them and never wanted to end up there herself. Mom was 81 years old and her broken femur was healing but she continued to refuse therapy. She was afraid she would not ever be able to leave the nursing home, but we encouraged her to work with the therapists so she could go home. She had always been sedentary and hated exercise so nothing had changed. I went to see her as often as I could. When I lived five minutes away, I went every day, but once I moved to Cleveland, I was forty-five minutes and 33 miles away. Eventually she was diagnosed with Alzheimer's. The condition progressively worsened but she did use a walker to get around for quite a while. She went through the usual swings of anger and depression. She forgot more and more. When I arrived to see her, I always reminded her saying, "Hi, Mom! It's me, Michelle, your daughter!" Even though her cognitive function was declining, her heart connection was not. I took her outdoors so she could get some fresh air and sunshine until the weather was no longer conducive. Then we sat in the side reception area on white wicker furniture and pretended we were at a tea house.

My sister continued to receive her treatments and from August 22, her birthday, to early December, my birthday, I didn't see her. When I would call to make arrangements to stop by when I was in town, her husband told me she was sleeping. The chemo was taking its toll. Then one day my brother and I got a call from her husband saying we should come to the hospital now. We didn't understand what was happening. We arrived and at the sight of us entering her room, my sister wailed and cried. I looked at her husband wondering what happened to her! She couldn't talk to us, she was already near death. She was taken home to receive hospice care for her last weeks on the Earth. I went to see her as often as I could, traveling to the classes I was teaching, then coming back afterward. We didn't know how long she would be here and after not seeing her for the past three months, I didn't want to waste any time. She couldn't speak, but she could still hear us. Her husband and Jeff turned her so she would be less inclined to get bed sores and the hospice people were compassionate and kind. For three weeks, I kept up this pace, going to see my sister, teaching in the City, going to see my mother and all in winter weather in a car with rear-wheel drive. It was treacherous, but I was *driven* to make these trips. During one afternoon visit with my sister, I was getting ready to leave to teach a class and come back. I told her that I was leaving and would be back soon—and that I loved her. She strained and said weakly but audibly, "I love you too." Those were the last words she ever spoke to me.

On December 19, my sister passed. I was beside myself with grief, losing my Big Sis that fought with me as children but bought me stylish clothes and gave me Christmas money when I was low on funds as adults. By now, Mom's condition with Alzheimer's was progressing and she had little hope of ever going back home. Dad wanted to bring her back home, but there wasn't anything workable with her care. His health was declining too, and at

89, he was enduring the stress of going to see her every day. With the loss of my sister, he was grieving and didn't know what to do. We discussed many times possibly taking Mom back home and trying to take care of her. But even in the nursing home, when the aides couldn't get to her in a timely manner and she made a mess in her clothes and bed, I helped clean her up. It was hard work and I already was working my job and filled with grief at the loss of my beautiful sister. Mom needed care 24/7 as well as proper medications that needed to be administered by a medical professional.

My brother and I managed to get Mom to our sister's funeral and she at first thought it was her own sister in the casket. I explained that it was Vickie and we'd lost her to cancer. She had a lucid moment and said, "This shouldn't happen that a child dies before her parents." With an aching heart, I tried to remain strong for my Mom. She was like an innocent child and needed protection from those with less understanding of her condition, or even that she had the condition.

The day after the funeral I went to my sister's graveside. There were flowers from the service lying over the mound with ribbons displaying qualities of her, like "Mother," "Grandmother," and so forth. I was looking at all the gold plastic words glued to the ribbons when I heard a large flock of geese coming. They sounded like they were having a party, all honking and screeching, flying low overhead. I looked up at them and had to smile. *Then I saw my sister's face fill the sky and I could feel her all around me—she was everywhere. She was smiling and conveyed to me that she was fine and happy and not to worry.* The geese were significant because her house was on the other side of some woods next to a Reiki client of mine. My client had several ponds on her large property and the geese used to love to stop there, leaving their debris and making it unpleasant for my client to use her yard. She would get her rifle and shoot into the air to scare the geese away. A couple of times I was standing in my sister's driveway when the flock of geese was flying overhead after my client shot her gun. My sister and I would laugh at the sight knowing what had happened. The geese over the cemetery were a sign and I believe she or Spirit arranged for them to fly overhead to get me to look up, both to see her smiling face but also for the inspiration that can come from simply "looking up."

As I continued to teach Yoga, I had an opportunity to buy a Yoga studio business in Medina just before my sister was diagnosed. I was busy making plans, pulling things together for this purchase and had started teaching at this studio in Medina. It was a rather long drive to the studio in Medina and while driving I prayed for a solution so that I wouldn't have to drive so far. I considered moving to Medina as well. As it turned out, the other party breached the contract we created and signed. I lost money on the deal, but during the weekend that happened, I received an email from a commercial realty company that wanted to lease space for a Yoga studio in Middleburg Heights. This was much closer anyway, so I let the Medina deal go and considered what I learned about the Yoga business from this woman as fair exchange for the down payment I had made and lost. She helped me build the confidence to open my own studio. I signed the lease with the company and was to open after the build-out in April of 2010. Even though my mother was in the nursing home and my father was aging, I felt I had the right to pursue a business career. So I proceeded to busily prepare for the grand opening. I had to work very hard, on top of already having worked hard to get the Medina studio going, which made a long period of enduring high stress levels.

In December, 2009, the day after my birthday, I had taught my usual 7 a.m. Clinic class in Strongsville and during the class I noticed my heart was racing a little like I had been running. I thought perhaps I was just out of shape, but after class, while I was driving down the freeway, my heart continued to race even faster. I thought it was going to pound its way out of my chest. I started to feel woozy so I pulled the car over to the side of the road, far enough so that there was no danger of being hit. I tried deep breathing, but that didn't seem to help and I became afraid. I called my friend that is a nurse and asked her advice. She suggested I take my pulse but when I tried, the beats were so fast and uneven that I couldn't count them. She recommended I call the emergency team. I called 9-1-1 and my heart continued to beat at break-neck speed.

Finally, the emergency medical team arrived and took me to the hospital. I waited in the emergency room for what seemed an eternity until the nurse came and performed some tests. My heart was in atrial fibrillation. I had a severe sinus infection as well. After a long while in the emergency unit, the came in nurse to give me an injection in my belly and the atrial fibrillation stopped almost immediately. I was taken to a hospital room and told I would remain overnight for observation. A doctor came and checked on me. John came too and such a blessing he was--by the time he arrived, I was watching television and filing my fingernails. He laughed when he walked in thinking I was going to be a basket case, all feeble and frail. I told him I was concerned about my car which was about 20 minutes from home—it was a safe distance from the highway, but I was concerned something still might happen to it. When he came back the next day to pick me up and drive me home, he told me he took a cab out to where my car was sitting and he drove it home. That's the kind of friend he is. He evoked an immense feeling of gratitude in me. Before I left the nurse came by and told me my potassium was slightly low and that it is possible the severe sinus infection had an impact since the bacteria could have drained down into my heart.

The doctor prescribed medication for me called a beta blocker. I checked into this and found that beta blockers suppress the adrenal glands. I did not want to *suppress* my adrenal glands--I wanted to *strengthen* them so I wouldn't have this reaction. I checked with a friend who is a family nurse practitioner that worked in ER at the Cleveland Clinic for ten years. She said I could back off the beta blockers without a problem. I started out on 100 mg. but became so sleepy I would nearly fall over even when seated! So the doctor reduced my dosage to 50 mg. It still made me sleepy. He also told me that I wouldn't be opening my Yoga Center due to the atrial fibrillation. Guidance showed me otherwise.

With further investigation, I discovered a product that could be purchased in a health food store called Adrenal Strength by MegaFood (the product contains Magnesium, necessary for heart health and muscles). After only one pill, which is made with organic food designed to address adrenal glands, I immediately felt better and continued taking them. I did have the start of an episode when I was headed out to my garage door a couple of weeks later. I started to feel the anxious feelings come over me and I immediately sent my energy down into the Center of the Earth and pulled it up into my body like I learned in Tom Kenyon's book, *The Hathor Material*. Immediately the feeling stopped and I was fine. So between sending my energy down into the Earth and pulling it up into my body and the Adrenal Strength, I have been well ever since. I did get a sinus infection one more time and felt the atrial fibrillation coming on, but getting Magnesium worked. I stayed on the product for about a year and felt my adrenal glands were doing well.

With my Center opening scheduled for just a few months away, my one astrologer told me that I have been killed in so many lifetimes for "putting myself out there" fighting for Humanity as a Buddhist and other lives where I was an activist that was assassinated, I was subconsciously terrified I would be killed in this life. I remained in a state of terror for a long time after I opened my Center, but by the time it was over at the end of the lease, well, ho hum.

The Yoga Center was beautiful. It was a 15-hours a day challenge which was not my idea of the Yogic lifestyle but it developed my assertiveness, ability to make decisions, ability to accept myself in spite of mistakes and the ability to overcome massive fear. It was not in a very good location and was very expensive with two studio rooms and two office rooms. We used one for massage or Reiki or Tarot readings and the other eventually became my office. Not long after I opened in April of 2010, I received a call from my oldest nephew, my sister's son. He told me that Jeff, my sister's middle son, had been in an accident and was killed almost instantly. It was less than two years since my sister passed and now Jeff was gone in September of 2010.

It was difficult to run the studio having lost my sister, I had not finished the grieving process yet when we lost Jeff. But they are together now and I'm sure getting into all kinds of mischief.

My mother was progressing with the Alzheimer's and I loved going to see her. I still announced myself when I went in and gave her hugs and kisses. She was so sweet to me, whether she knew who I was or not, I know our heart connection was still intact. I sang to her, John Denver's "Sunshine on My Shoulders Makes Me Happy" and a little ditty my grandmother taught us, "I Love You a Bushel and a Peck." She loved singing and sometimes we would go to the living room and sit at the piano. I didn't play but I could read music and knew where middle C was so could figure out simpler songs from the hymnal. She loved it. I would read to her and take her outdoors to see the Spring flowers. My Yoga classes were every Friday in town so I would teach at 10 a.m. and then after my sister was gone, my Dad and I met for lunch at the corner restaurant. We would laugh and talk and sit in the space in the front window watching the traffic go by. In winter we watched the snow fall. Dad was declining too, but these were precious times to be with him and love him. Childhood was too chaotic and messed up to enjoy my father, but now I had him all to myself. I had my father back. And Mom was becoming the Mom I never had as a kid too. I held her and learned to adore her. Even with Alzheimer's she had a sense of humor. Her words would get turned around sometimes. Someone gave her a stuffed animal snowman. When I asked her what she would name him, she replied, "Flow-snake." She meant Snowflake, of course, but the name stuck and I loved it. I saw her as more creative now in this condition.

When Mom got to the point where she couldn't eat very well by herself, I helped feed her when I was there during her lunch. It was bittersweet, watching her decline, but that condition is partly what I believe allowed her to be so sweet to me and allowed us to just love each other. I loved going to see her, I loved her. How far is that from when I wanted to murder her? Love changes things. All my Yoga practice and meditation, inner work, channeling, astrology, Tarot, and even my losses, all helped me return to my loving self.

My father's health declined with the stress of going to see my mother every day. Though she was sweet to me, she treated him very poorly. She constantly accused him of seeing another woman. She would even tell me he was seeing someone. I asked her, "Mom, he's 91 years old, what would he do with another woman?" She saw no logic in that and stuck to her belief. I think there was only one time in the seven years my mother lived in the nursing home that Dad had endured enough of her mean accusations and stayed home instead of seeing her.

We kids tried to get Dad to sell the house and move to a smaller place. We took him to a couple different assisted living facilities, but he said he would know when it was time to move. We knew he had no intention of moving his old, stubborn, German self out of that house. He seemed to have the attitude that he would rather die than leave the house. He would never stop driving either, even at age 91.

Dad needed to go to the hospital one day during the time my mother was in the nursing home. He had to have the full length of his abdominal aorta surgically replaced from his navel to his sternum. He had an aneurism that could pop at any moment. While he was recovering after surgery he contracted pneumonia and had to stay longer. After sufficient recovery, he was taken to the nursing home where my mother was for his rehabilitation.

One day when I went to visit him, he asked me to drive him to the nearby Barber Shop for a haircut. I agreed and helped him get ready. He was doing well and used a walker. When we got to the Barber Shop, I helped him out of the car and the barber even came out to hold onto him as he walked into the Shop. The barber held onto him tightly. Just something I noticed.

When we returned to the nursing home, I parked the car and helped Dad out and made sure he was holding his walker. I closed the car door and turned back toward Dad to see him – in seeming slow motion – falling backwards. I was seeing him fall in slow motion, but I couldn't move fast enough to catch him. He hit the back of his head on the pavement and couldn't get up. I felt horrible. I ran into the nursing home and told them at the nurses' station to call 9-1-1, my father had fallen. He was taken to the emergency room and returned after being checked and treated. His head hurt and his back hurt, so I offered him Reiki, but he wasn't really interested. He was feeling grumpy. After a while, I gave him privacy and went home. It was unusual to see my father grumpy—I felt the end coming.

The next day I came back to see my parents and learned that Dad had fallen in the hallway at the nursing home. His face was black and blue and he looked as though someone had beaten him up. All of this intensified his decline. It was so sad. He was miserable and unhappy. I visited with him for a while and then went to visit my mother.

During that same week, my brother and I both received a call from the nursing home. They had taken my father to the hospital with breathing problems. He had COPD from smoking as a young man and sailor and the doctor said that even though he had quit forty years prior, he smoked enough to cause the condition. My brother and his wife met me at the hospital and we intuitively felt Dad was transitioning to go Home. We stayed with him for quite a while and then my brother and his wife took a break. I stayed for a while longer but subsequently felt he might want some privacy for his transition. I went downstairs to get something to eat. When I came back, I could perceive his spirit leaving his body out through the top of his head. The respiratory therapist had put a mask over his face for him to breath in medicine. But I could see he wasn't breathing at all. I grabbed his hand and told him to squeeze, but he didn't. He was already on his way out. Such history we had together, forgiveness and close spiritual bond. When the nurse came in to take time of death, I told her in my fresh state of grief that my "Daddy" had just died. I never called him "Daddy" until that day. But that's how I still think of him. The doctor called the time 5:55 p.m. It was less than a year, May 30, 2011, since my nephew was killed. Memorial Day--Dad wanted us to remember him. How could we ever forget?

My brother and I weren't sure how to handle Mom in her condition with this new, major loss. We decided she should have the opportunity to visit Dad at the funeral parlor. We explained what we were doing and slowly wheeled her chair up to his casket. She didn't want to stand up, but we encouraged her so she could have closure. One never knows how or when a lucid moment will appear in an Alzheimer's patient. She stood for a second and then wanted to leave. After we returned to the nursing home, we talked a little bit and for a few moments she "got" it. I knew she did anyway, because of the heart connection. She grieved in her own way, though someone with more cognitive requirements might not agree. She asked where Dad was several times, especially since he was staying at the nursing home for rehab just before he passed over. We just told her he had work to do and would be away. She seemed comfortable with that. My poor mother, I could barely tolerate this crackling ache in my heart for her. In her old age, she seemed like such an innocent child. Perhaps the

Alzheimer's was somewhat of a protection for her, not having to live with these losses in an aware way.

After Dad was gone, within three weeks, his sister passed away too. My aunt was one of those people that always smiled. She was always upbeat and positive, even when her hips were causing her immense pain. But losing all these family members was breaking my heart. But then that's one way to open it wider, like cracking an egg and opening it so the contents fall out. How to endure my own life…

Now the moments I spent with my mother were even more precious than ever before. It was Spring again and I pushed her around town to see all the beautiful flowers. She couldn't see very well with macular degeneration, but I pushed her up close enough so she could lean over and smell the ones with fragrance. We would sit in the gazebo and watch people and traffic go by. We went around the corner for ice cream and ate it under the umbrella in front of the parlor. I wanted to do everything I could to make her feel loved and comfortable. Sometimes I would drive out twice a week, even though I was still running the Center. I had two more years on the lease, so I would do the best I could under the circumstances. I began to regret my choice, but I still felt it was Spirit directed. I was learning and growing and connecting with others in a way I had never experienced.

After Dad's passing, my brother and I had to clear out the house. I know many people have gone through this experience, but it was a major challenge. To make decisions on what to keep, what to give away, what to throw away, when it's someone else's hard earned possessions, is nothing short of agonizing. My parents had nearly seven decades of accumulation in the house and we had to clear all of it out. The house had to be sold in accordance with government requirements. My brother didn't feel well, but he and his wife were admirable in how they handled the situation. Since my sister was gone, my brother was next in line to handle the estate. We had two weeks to accomplish our task since a buyer won the bid on it almost as soon as it was placed on the market. Once we cleared everything out, the fellow that bought it started work preparing it for a rental. I had no desire to ever see it again now that it no longer belonged to my parents and I refuse to drive by it even now. The fellow seemed unkind, though it may just have been my vulnerability causing my perception. Poor Mom didn't even know we were getting rid of all her clothes and jewelry—everything. Perhaps for her, ignorance was bliss.

The Center, under all these circumstances was not doing very well. I never could pull together a cohesive team that shared the vision enough to invest time in even coming to staff meetings. Much of the time I was teaching 18 classes a week between the Cleveland Clinic and my Center, and this at age 65. With the recent deaths in my family, it was an opportunity to transcend the circumstances.

I continued to visit my mother as often as I could, my brother was not able to very often and she needed family around her. There were others in the family that stopped to see her, and the aides at the nursing home treated her with great love. She continued to decline though so we didn't go outdoors any more. I still sang to her and she would try to remember the words or the tune. I hugged her harder and kissed her cheeks, her forehead, her hands and giving her all I possibly could—and still felt that wasn't enough. I had grown to adore her. She declined at a slow, steady pace for a year and a half after Dad passed. As she got closer, she had stopped eating and the last day she sat up in her Brady chair before she was to go to bed permanently, she had a lucid moment. I could see the energy come into her eyes and light up her face, and she looked directly into my eyes—she emphatically said, "I love you! " Those were her last words to me, just like my sister. What a blessing those moments were, held deeply within my heart, and indelibly etched on the screen of my mind.

The last two weeks I went every day to see her, to be with her. I held her hand so she would know someone was there that loved her. I sang to her and softly stroked her arms and face. I played music that was designed for those preparing to pass over. The Hospice people were there 24 hours a day now and they were so compassionate. My darling mother was preparing to transition.

And so she did on October 29, 2012. I received a call at 4:30 in the morning that Mom had passed. I was with her the night before and wanted to be there when she left, but it wasn't meant to be. I was scheduled to give a 6:30 a.m. class that morning, regardless I drove to see her one more time before she went to the funeral home. She had been through so much pain and anguish in her life. A complete hysterectomy at age 23, her jaw mangled when she had her teeth pulled for dentures, she lost her father when she was 8 years old and more. But when I went that last time, ALL of the stress lines in her face were *gone*! She looked totally peaceful, a blessing to see. My brother couldn't make it over, so I went for both of us and explained to him about her countenance so he would be comforted too.

If my astrologer Buz Myers were alive today, I would be able to tell him that what he told me about my mother being a mirror for me and when I learned to love her, I would love myself, we did it. It took a long, long time, but Mom and I did it—together.

# 17 THE LAST CHAPTER – BUT A NEW BEGINNING

With only my twin brother left in my immediate family, I returned my attention to the Center in a state of grief to finish the work I started. I now had six months left on the lease. In checking emails and newsletters, I came across something that piqued my interest--but first a little background.

After Merishkan left, I sat on the living room floor next to my black cat and studied a book that a long ago friend had loaned me, a thick book with a broken binding. It was not an old book--it was dry and didn't hold together well. The material contained within its pages was beyond my comprehension. I tried to understand what I was reading, but it was about higher consciousness and I apparently needed to experience more soul growth to understand it. One portion of the book talked about the Vagus Nerve and how the ancient Yogis knew of its importance. I remember a graphic of the nerve, but I could not understand any more than that. I remember straining my brain in an attempt to understand what the authors were trying to convey. Suddenly my cat started stiff-legged cat-jumping and skittering all around the living room--she must have seen the ghost of a wildebeest to chase. She slid across the pages like she was surfing on paper, and scattered them all over the floor. I gathered them together and tried to put the book back together like Humpty-Dumpty, but I couldn't understand it well enough to connect the sentences from one page to another. And – amazingly enough – the pages had no numbers on them! Giving up, I eventually ditched the book.

In my ongoing studies over the years, I have followed Lee Carroll who channels Kryon (a contingency of Archangel Michael, I was with him in a dream), and Steve Rother who channels "the group." They are all angels working to raise consciousness and help Humanity to evolve. In the summer of 2012 then, about the time my mother was starting her transition, I saw Steve Rother's first offering of a course on the Vagus Nerve, much of the material channeled. My eyes nearly popped out of my head. I signed up for the course quickly.

## THE VAGUS NERVE CONNECTION TO ORGANS

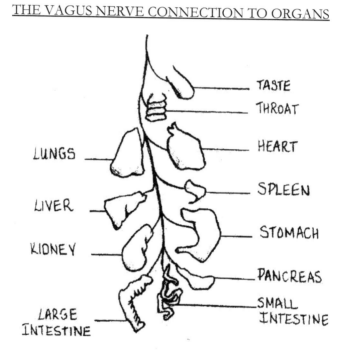

It was intriguing material and still a little difficult to understand, but I studied my notes and reviewed the videos from the course -- eventually it made sense. I also meditated on the Vagus Nerve and the Tube Torus (shown below) and received more information and clarity. Taking the course certified me to offer Vagus Nerve Activations for people. The Vagus Nerve is the longest cranial nerve in the body and impacts our calming of inflammation, heart coherence, telepathy, compassion, evolution and more. It is the nerve the sends messages to the brain to produce Oxytocin, the love and trust hormone. It can be damaged through trauma, emotional or physical—but it can also be activated and healed! I had already studied the Tube Torus and taught classes on the subject at the Center from the Tom Kenyon/Virginia Essene book, *The Hathor Material* and the Torus was included in the course on the Vagus Nerve. Things were coming together in my mind.

Briefly, the Tube Torus is the energy field around every living thing--a grid—it is a little more detailed than what most people consider the "aura."

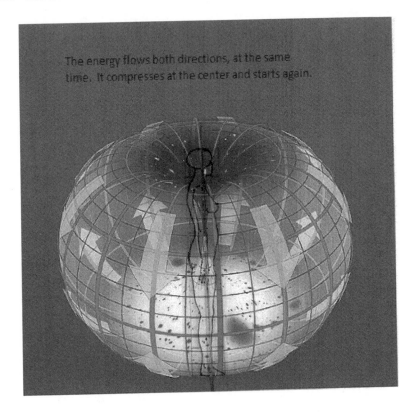

The energy flows both directions, at the same time. It compresses at the center and starts again.

The energy flows in from the Pranic Tube at the "north" and "south" ends similar to a straw-like extension up and out into the Universe, through the centerline of the body, and down into the center of the Earth. The arrows in the graphic depict the flow of energy. Emotions can get stuck in the energy gridlines, and wherever they intersect is another point of creativity. The emotions can be released from the grid which clears karma and expands awareness. It's what happens energetically when we release past-life trauma. I have been working with the Pranic Tube since the early 1980's as well as the aura. The Torus I learned about in mid-1990 from the Hathor book. I feel connected to the Hathors, especially knowing that I was a Pharaoh's daughter in Egypt (actually, my roommate John was the Pharaoh!) and connected with them during that life. They are like our brothers and sisters and have experienced dimensional shifts like the Earth and Humanity are experiencing now--and, they are providing assistance.

While I continued offering Yoga classes, Reiki appointments and all sorts of other workshops, the Center still did not prosper. I considered closing early, but it would not have made much difference. The lease had to be paid according to the contractual agreement whether the place was open or not. Even though I considered myself a good teacher, and a decent businesswoman, the fear I felt around such a daunting scenario deflected good things from coming in more freely. Love attracts, fear repulses. I thought I was a loving creature and sufficiently evolved to create a good experience, but I had not yet fully released my fears around being killed for my work in other lifetimes. It was another deep subconscious trauma to heal. I trudged on hoping people were receiving the healing that was being offered.

Sometimes when I was teaching Yoga, I saw students that were in the non-physical reality—ghosts if you will, and they were white. I could see them sitting cross-legged on the floor of the classroom, just like the other students. When I asked my guide about them, he told me I had a following from the other side of the veil because of what I do with energy. Too bad they couldn't pay for the classes! That's a joke, I know there is an energy exchange with them, and I am honored that they see fit to attend! My Reiki sessions have been interesting as well. The Angels attend and sometimes I see them clearly, and I know other Reiki practitioners experience their assistance. During one treatment I was giving a regular client, I saw Archangel Gabrielle at the end of the Reiki table holding a long brass trumpet to her mouth. She appeared human-like and was incredibly beautiful with waist-long wavy blonde hair and a full-length gown that appeared to be hunter green velvet with gold trim. She was blowing through her trumpet and panned both my client and me with it side to side. She relayed to me telepathically that with the energy she sent through her trumpet, (there was no audible sound) my client and I are to use the energy for creative writing! So here it is. This is my gift to you, with Angelic assistance!

The end of the lease was drawing near and I started to make plans to close. The angels were always present there, we were working together before opening and they acted as guardians all three years. I knew when I started the project that I would not remain there--I have other spiritual assignments and cannot be tied down to such a situation. But it was an amazing experience and it served me well in working through fears. At this point, even though the Center was not financially prosperous, I felt it served its purpose. And there are rewards for completing this clearing.

Being so busy all the time, my office at the Center had grown into a paper mountain and I didn't have time to wade through all the paperwork, so I packed it with all the rest of the supplies and furniture. Help magically appeared with students volunteering their time and Yoga-strengthened backs to move. Some of the furniture from my parent's home was housed at the Center, so it had to either be sold or placed in storage with the other furniture. I had enough furniture – with the lounge area that was so comfortable in between the two studio rooms – that would have filled an apartment. We packed it all and disseminated it to the storage unit, my home, or the Good Will. It was a huge task as moving always is, but all went smoothly. After everything was removed from the suite, I walked through stopping in each room to check for stray items. As I stood in each room, I was flooded with visions of the wonderful memories of events we held. Becky Bickford's South African Dance and Ecstatic Dance with Harry Pepper and other professional drummers providing live rhythms. Melissa Thomas Edington, a Radio City Music Hall celebrity Rockette bringing the party of Zumba, Rob Schwartz speaking on *Your Soul's Plan*, author and "modern-day Indiana Jones," Michael Tellinger speaking on his discoveries about ancient vanished civilizations at the southern tip of Africa, the many health fairs we had with Jan Lewis offering chair massage, Debi Balmert and Mike Pancoe teaching us about Zija nutrition and so much more. I stepped out the back door onto the deck remembering our many sunlit –or moonlit--classes overlooking the wetlands nature preserve where turkeys sauntered by, a snapping turtle laid her eggs next to the pond, and deer graced us with their presence. We even heard a pack of coyotes one night that brought a sense of wildness and magic. I thought I would feel sad walking through preparing to never return, but joy and appreciation were my main emotions. How wonderful it all was, even though a whirlwind. Each room "showed" me a review of all the beauty the Center held and shared. It was meant to be and it was meant to end.

The papers that littered my office now littered my home office. After closing, it took about a year and a half to clear it all up. But with that clearing came the full cleansing of my soul and the freedom to move forward with my spiritual assignments. It may seem anti-climactic to close and move on, but already I have created a workshop presentation on the Tube Torus and Vagus Nerve along with other information and Yoga sequences. I gave the workshop at a Yoga studio in Florida with the help of a friend with whom I graduated high school who teaches Pilates and Fitness there. When the traveling teaching job I had closed in 2005, there were two new women partners that magically appeared that filmed continuing education presentations for occupational and physical therapists. They are also located in Florida. We filmed a couple of four-hour Yoga DVDs for CEUs in 2005, and now in 2014 we collaborated again. We timed it so they could film my workshop while I was in Florida to give it at the Pilates and Yoga studio. I gave the workshop on the east side of Cleveland and the school psychologist that runs a learning center is interested in doing a study on the effects of the Vagus Nerve Activations on children. I took the second course on the Vagus Nerve in early 2014 with further certification and understanding. A woman at the workshop happened to be visiting Florida due to her mother's hospitalization. She is interested in having me come to her Pilates and Yoga studio in San Francisco to give the workshop for their teachers and resource library. My intention is also that this book will find its way into the hands of people that can benefit from the information and description of experiences recorded within.

As a last note about the return of my creativity, here is how I recognized it. My friend Barb and I were at my house visiting and I felt a presence arrive on the scene. This was after Merishkan and crew had left. I told Barb, my inner creative child as I will describe her, had returned and wanted to speak to Barb through me. I allowed myself to relax down into a meditative state and I was washed by the presence of the part of me that left when I went down the aisle in the Baptist Church with my parents. This part of me explained in great enthusiasm and unbridled power to Barb that *she had been with the whales all this time.* She said they protected her and now it was safe for her to join me in expressing through this incarnation. How interesting it is, the whales are another "totem" animal as explained in the Medicine Cards and that showed up in my card spread. The whales are in the position of the spread labeled as protecting my inner creativity. Perhaps we will continue that communication on this new path of direction. As for Coyote, I lost contact with her, but I heard she and her husband divorced. She changed yet again, into another person, providing him with his own initiation as she moved on. Such a service she is providing. Oddly enough, I'm truly grateful.

With the healing of my fears and traumas, facing my demons and embracing peace, the desire for which propelled me on this journey, I am now free. My intuition and psychic communication with my guides and creative self are flowing again and I have faith and newfound trust in Guidance and the Universe. I believe this is the peace that "passes all understanding." "Let there be peace on Earth, and let it begin with me."

It is done. It is so. Espavo!

# RESOURCES

Michelle's DVDs produced by Exploring Hand Therapy continuing education:

- **Yoga: Creative Clinical Wisdoms**
  http://www.liveconferences.com/product.asp?cid=265
- **Therapist in Your Pocket - Yoga The Five Tibetans**
  http://www.liveconferences.com/product.asp?cid=277

www.Lightworker.com – Paths2Empowerment/Overlight courses on the Vagus Nerve – Steve and Barbara Rother and "The Group" (channeled angels; Steve says "Espavo" means "thank you for taking your power.")

"Thrive" Movie Trailer http://ykr.be/1jeq2m8wba (explains the Tube Torus and Vector Equilibrium—movie available free online but without bonus features—can purchase full movie at this link); activist website: www.thrivemovement.com

ieoie, YouTube: "Torus Fun"
http://www.youtube.com/watch?v=u0eOuxJX36g The company, ieoie, (Rob Herman) is a graphic arts company in the Netherlands—copyrighted animation.

"What the Bleep Do We Know" DVD is an important video piece on how we attract each other energetically and how we create our reality. Candace B. Pert, Ph.D., Scientist/Author of *Molecules of Emotion* (shows how she found the receptor for the opiate molecules and shows how our emotions impact our health) is in this film. Science and Spirituality come together.

## Recommended Reading

"The Hathor Material" by Tom Kenyon and Virginia Essene (more on the tube torus and how to work with it)

"The Miracle Tree" by Monica Marcu, Pharm.D, Ph.D. – Moringa Tree

Zija – www.michellestar.myzija.com – made mostly with Moringa, the highest nutrient-rich botanical ON THE EARTH – Write michellestaryoga@gmail.com with questions.

"Complementary Therapies in Rehabilitation Evidence for Efficacy in Therapy, Prevention, and Wellness" – Author: Carol M. Davis (Chapter on Reiki: Chapter 14, page 235 by Sangeeta Singh, PhD; Chapter on Yoga Therapeutics: Chapter 10, page 157 by Matthew J. Taylor, MPT, RYT)

"The Polyvagal Theory" – Author: Stephen Porges (also see Youtube interview: http://www.youtube.com/watch?v=8tz146HQotY)

William Rand's Reiki website - www.Reiki.com

Mega Food – www.megafood.com – check out **Adrenal Strength** by MegaFood – awesome to replenish tired adrenal glands

To learn more about Michelle Star's workshops or services, visit her website at www.michellestaryoga.com.

# ABOUT THE AUTHOR

With a proven track record over a span of nearly 30 years, Michelle has received recognition as a committed professional in the field of Yoga and healing. Having conducted the Yoga therapy classes for the Cleveland Clinic's scientific study in 2000 entitled, "The Impact of Yoga on a Chronic Pain Population," Michelle demonstrated how Yoga can be a therapeutic tool for a range of physical and emotional challenges. (Study was orchestrated by Dr. Sonia Gaur, then a psychiatric resident).

The conclusion of the study revealed that "Yoga improves mood in chronic pain patients, leads to decreased medication use, and a decrease in pain severity. Results are statistically significant." Michelle taught for the Clinic employees for over 5 years, including during the time she operated her own double Yoga studio in Middleburg Heights, OH.

Much of Michelle's career has been spent traveling as a Yoga and Reiki instructor, leading classes and workshops in Ohio, Michigan, Indiana and Pennsylvania (and now Florida) since 1985. She offers Kripalu Yoga, giving instruction that touches all levels (physical, mental/emotional and spiritual). A Reiki practitioner and teacher since 1996, Michelle has attuned over a hundred Reiki practitioners.

In the past two years, Michelle has received elite certifications from Paths 2 Empowerment's OverLight series to facilitate Vagus Nerve Activations and offers appointments. She offers classes and workshops in Kripalu Yoga, Reiki, and Vagus Nerve Activations and offers readings and teaches Tarot as a creativity and self-knowledge tool. She is an affiliate with the Thrive Movement and a distributor for Zija International.

Michelle strives to promote personal empowerment and peace, one heart at a time.

Made in the USA
Middletown, DE
25 October 2015